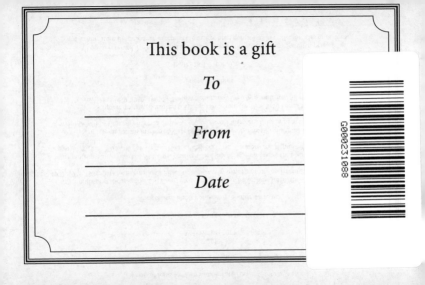

This book is a gift

To

_____

From

_____

Date

_____

G000231088

Words of Jesus for Everyday Living Pocket Companion

Published by Christian Art Publishers, PO Box 1599, Vereeniging, 1930, RSA

© 2011

First edition 2011

Designed by Christian Art Publishers

Images used under license from Shutterstock.com

Scripture quotations marked NIV are taken from the Holy Bible, New International Version® NIV®.
Copyright © 1973, 1978, 1984, 2011 by International Bible Society. Used by permission of Zondervan Publishing House. All rights reserved.

Scripture quotations marked NLT are taken from the Holy Bible, New Living Translation®, second edition.
Copyright © 1996, 2004, 2007 by Tyndale House Publishers, Inc., Carol Stream, Illinois 60188. All rights reserved.

Scripture quotations marked ESV are taken from the Holy Bible, English Standard Version.
Copyright © 2001 by Crossway Bibles, a division of Good News Publishers. Used by permission. All rights reserved.

Scripture quotations marked NKJV are taken from the New King James Version.
Copyright © 1979, 1980, 1982 by Thomas Nelson, Inc. Used by permission. All rights reserved.

Printed in China

ISBN 978-1-77036-936-8

14 15 16 17 18 19 20 21 22 23 – 12 11 10 9 8 7 6 5 4 3

WORDS OF JESUS

for everyday living

CHRISTIAN ART
PUBLISHERS

Introduction

"Remain in Me, as I also remain in you. No branch can bear fruit by itself; it must remain in the vine. Neither can you bear fruit unless you remain in Me."

– John 15:4

Jesus' words are a sanctuary to all who long for intimacy with their Savior. They remain eternal, providing guidelines for living our daily lives with godly character and to the glory of God.

This Pocket Companion edition of the words of Jesus will help you to grow and mature as a follower of Jesus by surrendering yourself to the profound value of His words. It will inspire, encourage and edify.

Contents

JESUS' WORDS
ABOUT HIMSELF

10

....
Jesus' Identity

"You know Me, and you know where I come from? But I have not come of My own accord. He who sent Me is true, and Him you do not know."

John 7:28 ESV

"No one has ever gone to heaven and returned. But the Son of Man has come down from heaven."

John 3:13 NLT

"You are from below; I am from above. You are of this world; I am not of this world."

John 8:23 ESV

"I am the Alpha and the Omega, the Beginning and the End, the First and the Last."

Rev. 22:13 NKJV

"I and the Father are one."

John 10:30 ESV

"Whoever has seen Me has seen the Father."

John 14:9 ESV

12

"I Am" Statements

"I am the bread of life. Whoever comes to Me will never go hungry, and whoever believes in Me will never be thirsty."

John 6:35 NIV

"I am the Son of God."

Matt. 27:43 NKJV

"I Am the Messiah!"

John 4:26 NLT

"I am the living bread that came down from heaven. Whoever eats this bread will live forever. This bread is My flesh, which I will give for the life of the world."

John 6:51 NIV

"I am the true bread that came down from heaven. Anyone who eats this bread will not die."

John 6:58 NLT

"I am the light of the world. Whoever follows Me will not walk in darkness, but will have the light of life."

John 8:12 ESV

"I Am" Statements

"As long as I am in the world, I am the light of the world."
John 9:5 NKJV

"I am the gate for the sheep."
John 10:7 NLT

"Yes, I am the gate. Those who come in through Me will be saved. They will come and go freely and will find good pastures."
John 10:9 NLT

"I am Jesus."
Acts 9:5 NKJV

"I am the good shepherd. The good shepherd lays down His life for the sheep."

John 10:11 ESV

"I am the good shepherd; I know My sheep and My sheep know Me."

John 10:14 NIV

"I am the resurrection and the life."

John 11:25 ESV

"I Am" Statements

"I am coming soon, bringing My reward with Me to repay all people according to their deeds."

Rev. 22:12 NLT

"I am the Alpha and the Omega, the Beginning and the End, the First and the Last."

Rev. 22:13 NKJV

"I am the root and the descendant of David, the bright morning star."

Rev. 22:16 ESV

"I will prove to you that the Son of Man has the authority on earth to forgive sins."

Matt. 9:6 NLT

"All authority in heaven and on earth has been given to Me."

Matt. 28:18 ESV

"I want you to know that the Son of Man has authority on earth to forgive sins."

Mark 2:10 NIV

"The Son of Man is lord of the Sabbath."

Luke 6:5 ESV

The Authority of Jesus

"I do nothing on My own authority, but speak just as the Father taught Me."

John 8:28 ESV

"No one can take My life from Me. I sacrifice it voluntarily. For I have the authority to lay it down when I want to and also to take it up again."

John 10:18 NLT

"I don't speak on My own authority. The Father who sent Me has commanded Me what to say and how to say it."

John 12:49 NLT

"All things have been handed over to Me by My Father, and no one knows the Son except the Father, and no one knows the Father except the Son and anyone to whom the Son chooses to reveal Him."

Matt. 11:27 ESV

"Whoever does the will of God is My brother and My sister and mother."

Mark 3:35 NKJV

"Whoever welcomes Me does not welcome Me but the one who sent Me."

Mark 9:37 NIV

Jesus and the Father

"Whoever receives Me receives Him who sent Me."

Luke 9:48 NKJV

"No one is good except God alone."

Luke 18:19 ESV

"The Son of Man will sit on the right hand of the power of God."

Luke 22:69 NKJV

"My Father has been working until now, and I have been working."

John 5:17 NKJV

"The Son can do nothing by Himself. He does only what He sees the Father doing. Whatever the Father does, the Son also does."

John 5:19 NLT

"The Father loves the Son, and shows Him all things that He Himself does; and He will show Him greater works than these."

John 5:20 NKJV

"I have come in My Father's name, and you do not receive Me; if another comes in his own name, him you will receive."

John 5:43 NKJV

Jesus and the Father

....

"The Father judges no one, but has committed all judgment to the Son, that all should honor the Son just as they honor the Father. He who does not honor the Son does not honor the Father who sent Him."

John 5:22-23 NKJV

"As the Father has life in Himself, so He has granted the Son to have life in Himself."

John 5:26 NKJV

"I can do nothing on My own. As I hear, I judge, and My judgment is just, because I seek not My own will but the will of Him who sent Me."

John 5:30 ESV

"The works that the Father has given Me to accomplish, the very works that I am doing, bear witness about Me that the Father has sent Me."

John 5:36 ESV

"I live because of the living Father who sent Me."

John 6:57 NLT

"I am not alone. I stand with the Father, who sent Me."

John 8:16 NIV

"I am the One who bears witness about Myself, and the Father who sent Me bears witness about Me."

John 8:18 ESV

"You know neither Me nor My Father. If you knew Me, you would know My Father also."

John 8:19 ESV

"He who sent Me is true; and I speak to the world those things which I heard from Him."

John 8:26 NKJV

"I do nothing on My own but say only what the Father taught Me."

John 8:28 NLT

"I have no wish to glorify Myself, God is going to glorify Me."

John 8:50 NLT

"Whoever sees Me sees Him who sent Me."

John 12:45 ESV

Jesus and the Father

"I am the way, and the truth, and the life. No one comes to the Father except through Me."

John 14:6 ESV

"Whoever accepts anyone I send accepts Me; and whoever accepts Me accepts the one who sent Me."

John 13:20 NIV

"The Son of Man is glorified and God is glorified in Him."

John 13:31 NIV

"God will glorify the Son in Himself."

John 13:32 NIV

"I am in the Father and the Father is in Me."

John 14:11 NIV

"I am going to the Father, for My Father is greater than I."

John 14:28 NKJV

"I will do what the Father requires of Me, so that the world will know that I love the Father."

John 14:31 NLT

"I am in My Father, and you in Me, and I in you."

John 14:20 ESV

Jesus and the Father

"I am the true vine, and My Father is the gardener."

John 15:1 NIV

"All things that the Father has are Mine."

John 16:15 NKJV

"O Father, glorify Me together with Yourself, with the glory which I had with You before the world was."

John 17:5 NKJV

"Make disciples of all the nations, baptizing them in the name of the Father and of the Son and of the Holy Spirit."

Matt. 28:19 NKJV

"Whoever blasphemes against the Holy Spirit never has forgiveness, but is guilty of an eternal sin."

Mark 3:29 ESV

"The Spirit of the Lord is upon Me, because He has anointed Me to proclaim good news to the poor."

Luke 4:18 ESV

Jesus and the Holy Spirit

"How much more will the heavenly Father give the Holy Spirit to those who ask Him!"

Luke 11:13 ESV

"Now I will send the Holy Spirit, just as My Father promised."

Luke 24:49 NLT

"No one can enter the kingdom of God unless they are born of water and the Spirit."

John 3:5 NIV

"It is the Spirit who gives life."

John 6:63 NKJV

"And I will ask the Father, and He will give you another advocate to help you and be with you forever – the Spirit of truth. The world cannot accept Him, because it neither sees Him nor knows Him. But you know Him, for He lives with you and will be in you. I will not leave you as orphans; I will come to you. Before long, the world will not see Me anymore, but you will see Me. Because I live, you also will live."

John 14:16-19 NIV

"The Advocate, the Holy Spirit, whom the Father will send in My name, will teach you all things and will remind you of everything I have said to you."

John 14:26 NIV

Jesus and the Holy Spirit

"When the Advocate comes, whom I will send to you from the Father – the Spirit of truth who goes out from the Father – He will testify about Me."

John 15:26 NIV

"It is for your good that I am going away. Unless I go away, the Advocate will not come to you; but if I go, I will send Him to you. When He comes, He will prove the world to be in the wrong about sin and righteousness and judgment."

John 16:7-8 NIV

"When He, the Spirit of truth, comes, He will guide you into all the truth. He will not speak on His own; He will speak only what He hears, and He will tell you what is yet to come. He will glorify Me because it is from Me that He will receive what He will make known to you. All that belongs to the Father is Mine. That is why I said the Spirit will receive from Me what He will make known to you."

John 16:13-15 NIV

"You will receive power when the Holy Spirit comes upon you. And you will be My witnesses, telling people about Me everywhere."

Acts 1:8 NLT

His Coming to Earth

"Do not think that I have come to abolish the Law or the Prophets; I have not come to abolish them but to fulfill them."
Matt. 5:17 ESV

"Those who are well have no need of a physician, but those who are sick. Go and learn what this means, 'I desire mercy, and not sacrifice.' For I came not to call the righteous, but sinners."
Matt. 9:12-13 ESV

"Do not think that I came to bring peace on earth. I did not come to bring peace but a sword."
Matt. 10:34 NKJV

"I will send My messenger ahead of You, who will prepare Your way before You."

Matt. 11:10 NIV

"The Son of Man did not come to be served, but to serve, and to give His life a ransom for many."

Matt. 20:28 NKJV

"I have not come to call the righteous, but sinners."

Mark 2:17 NIV

"I have appeared to you for this purpose, to make you a minister and a witness both of the things which you have seen and of the things which I will yet reveal to you."

Acts 26:16 NKJV

"The Spirit of the Lord is upon Me, because He has anointed Me to proclaim good news to the poor. He has sent Me to proclaim liberty to the captives and recovering of sight to the blind, to set at liberty those who are oppressed, to proclaim the year of the Lord's favor."

Luke 4:18-19 ESV

"I must preach the kingdom of God to the other cities also, because for this purpose I have been sent."

Luke 4:43 NKJV

"I was born and came into the world to testify to the truth. All who love the truth recognize that what I say is true."

John 18:37 NLT

"I brought glory to You here on earth by completing the work You gave Me to do."

John 17:4 NLT

"I have come to set the world on fire, and I wish it were already burning! I have a terrible baptism of suffering ahead of Me, and I am under a heavy burden until it is accomplished. Do you think I have come to bring peace to the earth? No, I have come to divide people against each other! From now on families will be split apart, three in favor of Me, and two against – or two in favor and three against."

Luke 12:49-52 NLT

"God did not send His Son into the world to condemn the world, but that the world through Him might be saved."

John 3:17 NKJV

"The Son of Man came to seek and to save the lost."

Luke 19:10 ESV

"My nourishment comes from doing the will of God, who sent Me, and from finishing His work."

John 4:34 NLT

"I have come in My Father's name."

John 5:43 NKJV

His Coming to Earth

"I have come down from heaven, not to do My own will but the will of Him who sent Me."

John 6:38 ESV

"This is the will of the Father who sent Me, that of all He has given Me I should lose nothing, but should raise it up at the last day."

John 6:39 NKJV

"I came from God and I am here. I came not of My own accord, but He sent Me."

John 8:42 ESV

"For judgment I have come into this world, so that the blind will see and those who see will become blind."

John 9:39 NIV

"I have come that they may have life, and have it to the full."

John 10:10 NIV

"Now My soul is troubled, and what shall I say? 'Father, save Me from this hour'? No, it was for this very reason I came to this hour. Father, glorify Your name!"

John 12:27-28 NIV

His Coming to Earth

....

"I have come into the world as a light, so that no one who believes in Me should stay in darkness."

John 12:46 NIV

"I have come to set the world on fire, and I wish it were already burning!"

Luke 12:49 NLT

"I did not come to judge the world, but to save the world."

John 12:47 NIV

JESUS' WORDS ABOUT FOLLOWING HIM

"Follow Me, and I will make you fishers of men."

Matt. 4:19 NKJV

"If you want to be perfect, go, sell your possessions and give to the poor, and you will have treasure in heaven. Then come, follow Me."

Matt. 19:21 NIV

"Follow Me, and let the dead bury their own dead."

Matt. 8:22 NKJV

"Make disciples of all nations, baptizing them in the name of the Father and of the Son and of the Holy Spirit."

Matt. 28:19 ESV

"Follow Me and be My disciple."

Mark 2:14 NLT

"Whoever wants to be My disciple must deny themselves and take up their cross and follow Me."

Mark 8:34 NIV

"Go into all the world and preach the Good News to everyone."

Mark 16:15 NLT

"Stay dressed for action and keep your lamps burning."

Luke 12:35 ESV

"If you want to be My disciple, you must hate everyone else by comparison ... even your own life. Otherwise, you cannot be My disciple."

Luke 14:26 NLT

"Those of you who do not give up everything you have cannot be My disciples."

Luke 14:33 NIV

"The knowledge of the secrets of the kingdom of heaven has been given to you."

Matt. 13:11 NIV

"When the Son of Man sits on the throne of His glory, you who have followed Me will also sit on twelve thrones."

Matt. 19:28 NKJV

"There is no one who has left house or brothers or sisters or father or mother or wife or children or lands, for My sake and the gospel's, who shall not receive a hundredfold."

Mark 10:29-30 NKJV

Promises to His Followers

"I have given you authority to trample on snakes and scorpions and to overcome all the power of the enemy; nothing will harm you."

Luke 10:19 NIV

"I have prayed for you that your faith may not fail."

Luke 22:32 ESV

"Whoever serves Me must follow Me; and where I am, My servant also will be. My Father will honor the one who serves Me."

John 12:26 NIV

"Remain in Me, and I will remain in you."

John 15:4 NLT

"You will receive power when the Holy Spirit comes upon you. And you will be My witnesses, telling people about Me everywhere."

Acts 1:8 NLT

"All those the Father gives Me will come to Me, and whoever comes to Me I will never drive away."

John 6:37 NIV

About His Followers

"You are the salt of the earth."

Matt. 5:13 NIV

"You are the light of the world."

Matt. 5:14 NIV

"The harvest is plentiful but the workers are few."

Matt. 9:37 NIV

"If anyone will not welcome you or listen to your words, leave that home or town and shake the dust off your feet."

Matt. 10:14 NIV

"Every teacher of the law who has become a disciple in the kingdom of heaven is like the owner of a house who brings out of his storeroom new treasures as well as old."

Matt. 13:52 NIV

"I am sending you out like lambs among wolves."

Luke 10:3 NIV

"Consider the ravens, for they neither sow nor reap, which have neither storehouse nor barn; and God feeds them. Of how much more value are you than the birds?"

Luke 12:24 NKJV

About His Followers

"If you abide in My word, you are My disciples indeed."

John 8:31 NKJV

"Everyone will know that you are My disciples, if you love one another."

John 13:35 NIV

"When you produce much fruit, you are My true disciples."

John 15:8 NLT

"You did not choose Me, but I chose you and appointed you that you should go and bear fruit."

John 15:16 NKJV

"You will be handed over to be persecuted and put to death, and you will be hated by all nations because of Me."

Matt. 24:9 NIV

"You will stand trial before governors and kings because you are My followers. But this will be your opportunity to tell them about Me."

Mark 13:9 NLT

"Everyone will hate you because you are My followers."

Mark 13:13 NLT

"Whoever is not against you is for you."

Luke 9:50 NIV

"I am the vine; you are the branches. If you remain in Me and I in you, you will bear much fruit; apart from Me you can do nothing."

John 15:5 NIV

"Whoever is not with Me is against Me."

Luke 11:23 ESV

"Blessed are those who are persecuted for righteousness' sake, for theirs is the kingdom of heaven."

Matt. 5:10 ESV

"Blessed are you when people insult you, persecute you and falsely say all kinds of evil against you because of Me."

Matt. 5:11 NIV

"Rejoice and be glad, because great is your reward in heaven, for in the same way they persecuted the prophets who were before you."

Matt. 5:12 NIV

"Love your enemies and pray for those who persecute you."

Matt. 5:44 ESV

"I am sending you out like sheep among wolves. Therefore be as shrewd as snakes and as innocent as doves."

Matt. 10:16 NIV

"I will send them prophets and apostles, some of whom they will kill and others they will persecute."

Luke 11:49 NIV

"Be on your guard; you will be handed over to the local councils and be flogged in the synagogues. On My account you will be brought before governors and kings as witnesses to them and to the Gentiles. But when they arrest you, do not worry about what to say or how to say it. At that time you will be given what to say, for it will not be you speaking, but the Spirit of your Father speaking through you."

Matt. 10:17-20 NIV

Persecution of His Followers

"Brother will betray brother to death, and a father his child; children will rebel against their parents and have them put to death. You will be hated by everyone because of Me, but the one who stands firm to the end will be saved. When you are persecuted in one place, flee to another. Truly I tell you, you will not finish going through the towns of Israel before the Son of Man comes."

Matt. 10:21-23 NIV

"If they persecuted Me, they will also persecute you. If they kept My word, they will keep yours also."

John 15:20 NKJV

"Behold, the hour is coming, indeed it has come, when you will be scattered, each to his own home, and will leave Me alone. Yet I am not alone, for the Father is with Me. I have said these things to you, that in Me you may have peace. In the world you will have tribulation. But take heart; I have overcome the world."

John 16:32-33 ESV

"I am Jesus, the one you are persecuting!"

Acts 9:5 NLT

Doing God's Will

"We must carry out all that God requires."

Matt. 3:15 NLT

"Your kingdom come, Your will be done, on earth as it is in heaven."

Matt. 6:10 ESV

"It is not the will of your Father who is in heaven that one of these little ones should perish."

Matt. 18:14 NKJV

"Whoever does the will of God is My brother and My sister and mother."

Mark 3:35 NKJV

"My nourishment comes from doing the will of God, who sent Me, and from finishing His work."

John 4:34 NLT

"I have come down from heaven, not to do My own will, but the will of Him who sent Me."

John 6:38 NKJV

Doing God's Will

"My Father's will is that everyone who looks to the Son and believes in Him shall have eternal life."

John 6:40 NIV

"Anyone who chooses to do the will of God will find out whether My teaching comes from God or whether I speak on My own."

John 7:17 NIV

"As the Father has sent Me, I also send you."

John 20:21 NKJV

"Remain in Me, as I also remain in you. No branch can bear fruit by itself; it must remain in the vine. Neither can you bear fruit unless you remain in Me."

John 15:4 NIV

"By this My Father is glorified, that you bear much fruit."

John 15:8 NKJV

"You didn't choose Me. I chose you. I appointed you to go and produce lasting fruit."

John 15:16 NLT

Generosity

"Give to those who ask, and don't turn away from those who want to borrow."

Matt. 5:42 NLT

"When you do a charitable deed, do not let your left hand know what your right hand is doing, that your charitable deed may be in secret; and your Father who sees in secret will Himself reward you openly."

Matt. 6:3–4 NKJV

"Where your treasure is, there your heart will be also."

Matt. 6:21 NKJV

"Freely you have received, freely give."

Matt. 10:8 NKJV

"Be merciful, just as your Father is merciful."

Luke 6:36 NIV

"Give, and it will be given to you: good measure, pressed down, shaken together, and running over will be put into your bosom. For with the same measure that you use, it will be measured back to you."

Luke 6:38 NKJV

Generosity

"Be generous to the poor, and everything will be clean for you."

Luke 11:41 NIV

"Beware! Guard against every kind of greed. Life is not measured by how much you own."

Luke 12:15 NLT

"Use worldly wealth to gain friends for yourselves, so that when it is gone, you will be welcomed into eternal dwellings."

Luke 16:9 NIV

"Let what you say be simply 'Yes' or 'No'; anything more than this comes from evil."

Matt. 5:37 ESV

"One who is dishonest in a very little is also dishonest in much."

Luke 16:10 ESV

"When the Spirit of truth comes, He will guide you into all the truth."

John 16:13 ESV

Being Hospitable

"Whatever you did for one of the least of these brothers and sisters of Mine, you did for Me."

Matt. 25:40 NIV

"Anyone who gives you a cup of water in My name because you belong to the Messiah will certainly not lose their reward."

Mark 9:41 NIV

"When you give a feast, invite the poor, the crippled, the lame, the blind, and you will be blessed, because they cannot repay you."

Luke 14:13-14 ESV

"When you fast, do not be like the hypocrites, with a sad countenance. For they disfigure their faces that they may appear to men to be fasting. Assuredly, I say to you, they have their reward. But you, when you fast, anoint your head and wash your face, so that you do not appear to men to be fasting."

Matt. 6:16-18 NKJV

"You hypocrites! Isaiah was right when he prophesied about you: 'These people honor Me with their lips, but their hearts are far from Me. They worship Me in vain; their teachings are merely human rules.'"

Matt. 15:7-9 NIV

Hypocrisy

"The teachers of the law and the Pharisees sit in Moses' seat. So you must be careful to do everything they tell you. But do not do what they do, for they do not practice what they preach. They tie up heavy, cumbersome loads and put them on other people's shoulders, but they themselves are not willing to lift a finger to move them."

Matt. 23:2-4 NIV

"Woe to you, teachers of the law and Pharisees, you hypocrites! You shut the door of the kingdom of heaven in people's faces. You yourselves do not enter, nor will you let those enter who are trying to."

Matt. 23:13 NIV

"What sorrow awaits you teachers of religious law and you Pharisees. Hypocrites! For you are careful to tithe even the tiniest income from your herb gardens, but you ignore the more important aspects of the law – justice, mercy, and faith. You should tithe, yes, but do not neglect the more important things. Blind guides!"

Matt. 23:23-24 NLT

"Hypocrite! First remove the plank from your own eye, and then you will see clearly to remove the speck from your brother's eye."

Matt. 7:5 NKJV

"God blesses those who are humble, for they will inherit the whole earth."

Matt. 5:5 NLT

"Anyone who becomes as humble as this little child is the greatest in the Kingdom of Heaven."

Matt. 18:4 NLT

"Whoever wants to be a leader among you must be your servant."

Matt. 20:26 NLT

"The greatest among you shall be your servant."

Matt. 23:11 ESV

"Whoever exalts himself will be humbled, and whoever humbles himself will be exalted."

Matt. 23:12 ESV

"Take my yoke upon you. Let Me teach you because I am humble and gentle at heart, and you will find rest for your souls."

Matt. 11:29 NLT

Humility

"When someone invites you to a wedding feast, do not take the place of honor, for a person more distinguished than you may have been invited. If so, the host who invited both of you will come and say to you, 'Give this person your seat.' Then, humiliated, you will have to take the least important place. But when you are invited, take the lowest place, so that when your host comes, he will say to you, 'Friend, move up to a better place.' Then you will be honored in the presence of all the other guests."

Luke 14:8-10 NIV

Jesus said to the Pharisees, "You are the ones who justify yourselves in the eyes of others, but God knows your hearts. What people value highly is detestable in God's sight."

Luke 16:15 NIV

"You have heard that it was said, 'You shall love your neighbor and hate your enemy.' But I say to you, love your enemies, bless those who curse you, do good to those who hate you, and pray for those who spitefully use you and persecute you."

Matt. 5:43-44 NKJV

"Bless those who curse you. Pray for those who hurt you."

Luke 6:28 NLT

"If someone slaps you on one cheek, turn to them the other also. If someone takes your coat, do not withhold your shirt from them. Give to everyone who asks you, and if anyone takes what belongs to you, do not demand it back."

Luke 6:29-30 NIV

"Do to others as you would have them do to you."

Luke 6:31 NIV

"But if you love those who love you, what credit is that to you? For even sinners love those who love them. And if you do good to those who do good to you, what credit is that to you? For even sinners do the same. And if you lend to those from whom you hope to receive back, what credit is that to you? For even sinners lend to sinners to receive as much back."

Luke 6:32-34 NKJV

"Love your enemies! Do good to them."

Luke 6:35 NLT

Loving Others

....

"Your love for one another will prove to the world that you are My disciples."

John 13:35 NLT

"Love one another as I have loved you."

John 15:12 NKJV

"Greater love has no one than this, than to lay down one's life for his friends. You are My friends if you do whatever I command you."

John 15:13-14 NKJV

"Whoever loves father or mother more than Me is not worthy of Me, and whoever loves son or daughter more than Me is not worthy of Me."

Matt. 10:37 ESV

"You shall love the Lord your God with all your heart and with all your soul and with all your mind. This is the great and first commandment. And a second is like it: You shall love your neighbor as yourself."

Matt. 22:37-39 ESV

"Whoever has My commandments and keeps them, he it is who loves Me. And he who loves Me will be loved by My Father, and I will love him and manifest Myself to him."

John 14:21 NKJV

"My sheep hear My voice, and I know them, and they follow Me."

John 10:27 NKJV

"Blessed are the merciful, for they shall receive mercy."

Matt. 5:7 ESV

"I desire mercy, and not sacrifice."

Matt. 12:7 ESV

"Be merciful, just as your Father is merciful."

Luke 6:36 NIV

Obedience

"If anyone forces you to go one mile, go with them two miles."
Matt. 5:41 NIV

"Not everyone who says to Me, 'Lord, Lord,' will enter the kingdom of heaven, but the one who does the will of My Father who is in heaven."
Matt. 7:21 ESV

"Whoever has ears, let them hear."
Matt. 13:9 NIV

"If you abide in My word, you are My disciples indeed."

John 8:31 NKJV

"Whoever obeys My word will never see death."

John 8:51 NIV

"If you love Me, obey My commandments."

John 14:15 NLT

Peace

....

"Blessed are the peacemakers, for they will be called children of God."

Matt. 5:9 NIV

"Peace I leave with you, My peace I give to you."

John 14:27 NKJV

"Whenever you enter someone's home, first say, 'May God's peace be on this house.' If those who live there are peaceful, the blessing will stand; if they are not, the blessing will return to you."

Luke 10:5-6 NLT

"Because you believed, it has happened."

Matt. 8:13 NLT

"If you had faith even as small as a mustard seed, you could say to this mountain, 'Move from here to there,' and it would move. Nothing would be impossible."

Matt. 17:20 NLT

"Because of your faith, it will happen."

Matt. 9:29 NLT

"Great is your faith! Be it done for you as you desire."

Matt. 15:28 ESV

Faith

....

"If you have faith and don't doubt, you can do things like this and much more."

Matt. 21:21 NLT

"If you believe, you will receive whatever you ask for in prayer."

Matt. 21:22 NIV

"Why are you so afraid? Have you still no faith?"

Mark 4:40 ESV

"Don't be afraid. Just have faith."

Mark 5:36 NLT

"Anything is possible if a person believes."

Mark 9:23 NLT

"All things are possible with God."

Mark 10:27 ESV

"Have faith in God."

Mark 11:22 NKJV

"If anyone says to this mountain, 'Go, throw yourself into the sea,' and does not doubt in their heart but believes that what they say will happen, it will be done for them."

Mark 11:23 NIV

Faith

"You can pray for anything, and if you believe that you've received it, it will be yours."

Mark 11:24 NLT

"I have not found such great faith even in Israel!"

Luke 7:9 NIV

"Your faith has saved you. Go in peace."

Luke 7:50 NKJV

"If I have told you earthly things and you do not believe, how can you believe if I tell you heavenly things?"

John 3:12 ESV

"Will you never believe in Me unless you see miraculous signs and wonders?"

John 4:48 NLT

"Believe in the one He has sent."

John 6:29 NIV

"He who believes in Me has everlasting life."

John 6:47 NKJV

"Whoever believes in Me, as Scripture has said, rivers of living water will flow from within them."

John 7:38 NIV

"Believe in God; believe also in Me."

John 14:1 ESV

"Believe because of the work you have seen Me do."

John 14:11 NLT

"Whoever believes in Me will do the works I have been doing, and they will do even greater things than these."

John 14:12 NIV

"Stop doubting and believe."

John 20:27 NIV

"Blessed are those who have not seen and yet have believed."

John 20:29 NIV

"Blessed are the pure in heart, for they shall see God."

Matt. 5:8 ESV

"Whoever does what is true comes to the light, so that it may be clearly seen that his works have been carried out in God."

John 3:21 ESV

"I know all the things you do. I have seen your love, your faith, your service, and your patient endurance."

Rev. 2:19 NLT

"It is fitting for us to fulfill all righteousness."

Matt. 3:15 ESV

"Blessed are those who hunger and thirst for righteousness, for they shall be satisfied."

Matt. 5:6 ESV

"Blessed are those who are persecuted for righteousness' sake."

Matt. 5:10 ESV

Righteousness

"Unless your righteousness is better than the righteousness of the teachers of religious law and the Pharisees, you will never enter the Kingdom of Heaven!"

Matt. 5:20 NLT

"Beware of practicing your righteousness before other people in order to be seen by them, for then you will have no reward from your Father who is in heaven."

Matt. 6:1 ESV

"The righteous will shine like the sun in the Kingdom of their Father."

Matt. 13:43 ESV

"Your eye is the lamp of your body. When your eye is healthy, your whole body is full of light, but when it is bad, your body is full of darkness. Therefore be careful lest the light in you be darkness. If then your whole body is full of light, having no part dark, it will be wholly bright."

Luke 11:34-36 ESV

"Seek first the Kingdom of God and His righteousness, and all these things shall be added to you."

Matt. 6:33 NIV

"God is spirit, and those who worship Him must worship in spirit and truth."

John 4:24 ESV

"Everyone on the side of truth listens to Me."

John 18:37 NIV

"You shall know the truth, and the truth shall make you free."

John 8:32 NKJV

"The greatest among you must be a servant."

Matt. 23:11 NLT

"Anyone who wants to be first must be the very last, and the servant of all."

Mark 9:35 NIV

"Be dressed for service and keep your lamps burning."

Luke 12:35 NLT

"It is more blessed to give than to receive."

Acts 20:35 NKJV

"Whoever serves Me must follow Me; and where I am, My servant also will be. My Father will honor the one who serves Me."

John 12:26 NIV

"A servant is not greater than his master."

John 15:20 NKJV

"No one can serve two masters; for either he will hate the one and love the other, or else he will be loyal to the one and despise the other."

Matt. 6:24 NKJV

"Every matter may be established by the testimony of two or three witnesses."

Matt. 18:16 NIV

"The testimony of two people is true."

John 8:17 ESV

"All things that I heard from My Father I have made known to you."

John 15:15 NKJV

"You also must testify."

John 15:27 NIV

"The closer you listen, the more understanding you will be given – and you will receive even more."

Mark 4:24 NLT

"To those who listen to My teaching, more understanding will be given. But for those who are not listening, even what little understanding they have will be taken away from them."

Mark 4:25 NLT

"Anyone who listens to My teaching and follows it is wise."

Matt. 7:24 NLT

"Anyone who hears My teaching and doesn't obey it is foolish."

Matt. 7:26 NLT

"I will give you a mouth and wisdom which all your adversaries will not be able to contradict or resist."

Luke 21:15 NKJV

"The spirit indeed is willing, but the flesh is weak."

Matt. 26:41 ESV

"Take courage! I am here!"

Mark 6:50 NLT

"In this world you will have trouble. But take heart! I have overcome the world."

John 16:33 NIV

"So don't be afraid; you are worth more that many sparrows."

Matt. 10:31 NIV

"Do not be afraid."

Matt. 14:27 ESV

"Have no fear."

Matt 17:7 ESV

"You have little faith, why are you so afraid? "

Matt. 8:26 NIV

"Do not be afraid, but go on speaking and do not be silent, for I am with you, and no one will attack you to harm you."

Acts 18:9-10 ESV

"Do not be afraid; I am the First and the Last."

Rev. 1:17 NKJV

"Do not fear any of those things which you are about to suffer."

Rev. 2:10 NKJV

"If the world hates you, remember that it hated Me first."

John 15:18 NLT

"Whoever hates Me hates My Father also."

John 15:23 ESV

"The world cannot hate you, but it hates Me because I testify of it that its works are evil."

John 7:7 NKJV

"Rejoice and be glad, for your reward is great in heaven."

Matt. 5:12 ESV

"Blessed are you who weep now, for you will laugh."

Luke 6:21 NIV

"Be happy! Yes, leap for joy! For a great reward awaits you in heaven."

Luke 6:23 NLT

"Rejoice because your names are written in heaven."

Luke 10:20 NKJV

"I say to you that you will weep and lament, but the world will rejoice; and you will be sorrowful, but your sorrow will be turned into joy."

John 16:20 NKJV

"Ask, and you will receive, that your joy may be full."

John 16:24 NKJV

Love

....

"Love your enemies and pray for those who persecute you."
Matt. 5:44 ESV

"Love your neighbor as yourself."
Matt. 22:39 NKJV

"Bless those who curse you. Pray for those who hurt you."
Luke 6:28 NLT

"Do to others as you would have them do to you."
Luke 6:31 NIV

"Love your enemies! Do good to them."

Luke 6:35 NLT

"Your love for one another will prove to the world that you are My disciples."

John 13:35 NLT

"Love one another as I have loved you."

John 15:12 NKJV

"Let your good deeds shine out for all to see, so that everyone will praise your heavenly Father."

Matt. 5:16 NLT

"Sickness will not end in death. No, it is for God's glory so that God's Son may be glorified through it."

John 11:4 NIV

"Father, glorify Your name."

John 12:28 NKJV

"I will do whatever you ask in My name, so that the Father may be glorified in the Son."

John 14:13 NIV

"The Son of Man is glorified, and God is glorified in Him. If God is glorified in Him, God will also glorify Him in Himself, and glorify Him immediately."

John 13:31-32 NKJV

"This is to My Father's glory, that you bear much fruit, showing yourselves to be My disciples."

John 15:8 NIV

Worry

"Do not worry about your life, what you will eat or drink; or about your body, what you will wear."

Matt. 6:25 NIV

"Don't worry about tomorrow, for tomorrow will bring its own worries."

Matt. 6:34 NLT

"Come to Me, all you who are weary and burdened, and I will give you rest."

Matt. 11:28 NIV

"Take My yoke upon you and learn from Me, for I am gentle and lowly in heart, and you will find rest for your souls."

Matt. 11:29 NKJV

"You are worried and upset about many things, but few things are needed – or indeed only one."

Luke 10:41-42 NIV

"Can all your worries add a single moment to your life?"

Luke 12:25 NLT

"Your Father already knows your needs."

Luke 12:30 NLT

Sin

"Everyone who looks at a woman with lustful intent has already committed adultery with her in his heart."

Matt. 5:28 ESV

"Out of the heart come evil thoughts – murder, adultery, sexual immorality, theft, false testimony, slander."

Matt. 15:19 NIV

"If your hand or foot causes you to sin, cut it off."

Matt. 18:8 NKJV

"If your eye causes you to sin, tear it out and throw it away."

Matt. 18:9 NKJV

"If you hold anything against anyone, forgive them, so that your Father in heaven may forgive you your sins."

Mark 11:25 NKJV

"Whoever commits sin is a slave of sin."

John 8:34 NKJV

"The world's sin is that it refuses to believe in Me."

John 16:9 ESV

"Your sins are forgiven."

Luke 7:48 NKJV

Repentance

"Repent of your sins and turn to God."

Matt. 4:17 NLT

"Repent, and believe in the gospel."

Mark 1:15 NKJV

"There is forgiveness of sins for all who repent."

Luke 24:47 NLT

"There will be more joy in heaven over one sinner who repents than over ninety-nine righteous persons who need no repentance."

Luke 15:7 ESV

"There is joy in the presence of God's angels when even one sinner repents."

Luke 15:10 NLT

"Open their eyes, so that they may turn from darkness to light and from the power of Satan to God."

Acts 26:18 NKJV

"Remember therefore from where you have fallen; repent, and do the works you did at first."

Rev. 2:5 ESV

Repentance

"Repent, or else I will come to you quickly and will fight against them with the sword of My mouth."

Rev. 2:16 NKJV

"Remember therefore how you have received and heard; hold fast and repent."

Rev. 3:3 NKJV

"Be zealous and repent."

Rev. 3:19 NKJV

"If you forgive those who sin against you, your heavenly Father will forgive you."

Matt. 6:14 NLT

"If you do not forgive others their trespasses, neither will your Father forgive your trespasses."

Matt. 6:15 ESV

"Be encouraged, My child! Your sins are forgiven."

Matt. 9:2 NLT

God's Forgiveness

"This is My blood of the covenant, which is poured out for many for the forgiveness of sins."

Matt. 26:28 ESV

"All sins will be forgiven the children of man, and whatever blasphemies they utter."

Mark 3:28 ESV

"Forgive, and you will be forgiven."

Luke 6:37 NKJV

"There is forgiveness of sins for all who repent."

Luke 24:47 NLT

"If you forgive anyone's sins, their sins are forgiven; if you do not forgive them, they are not forgiven."

John 20:23 NIV

"They will receive forgiveness for their sins and be given a place among God's people, who are set apart by faith in Me."

Acts 26:18 NLT

Judgment

"Anyone who is angry with a brother or sister will be subject to judgment."

Matt. 5:22 NIV

"If you had known what this means, 'I desire mercy, and not sacrifice,' you would not have condemned the guiltless."

Matt. 12:7 ESV

"By your words you will be acquitted, and by your words you will be condemned."

Matt. 12:37 NIV

"With the measure you use, it will be measured to you – and even more."

Mark 4:24 NIV

"Do not judge others, and you will not be judged."

Luke 6:37 NLT

"Do not judge by appearances, but judge with right judgment."

John 7:24 ESV

"I have much to say about you and much to condemn, but I won't."

John 8:26 NLT

Money and Possessions

"It is easier for a camel to go through the eye of a needle than for a rich man to enter the kingdom of God."

Matt. 19:24 NKJV

"Everyone who has given up houses or brothers or sisters or father or mother or children or property, for My sake, will receive a hundred times as much in return and will inherit eternal life."

Matt. 19:29 NLT

"Go and sell all your possessions and give the money to the poor, and you will have treasure in heaven."

Mark 10:21 NLT

"What sorrow awaits you who are rich, for you have your only happiness now."

Luke 6:24 NLT

"To the one who has, more will be given, and from the one who has not, even what he thinks that he has will be taken away."

Luke 8:18 ESV

"Beware! Guard against every kind of greed. Life is not measured by how much you own."

Luke 12:15 NLT

Money and Possessions

"Sell your possessions, and give to the needy."

Luke 12:33 ESV

"Where your treasure is, there your heart will be also."

Luke 12:34 NKJV

"You cannot become My disciple without giving up everything you own."

Luke 14:33 NLT

"You will always have the poor among you, but you will not always have Me."

John 12:8 NLT

"Judgment will fall on this very generation."

Matt. 23:36 NLT

"Someone who does not know, and then does something wrong, will be punished only lightly."

Luke 12:48 NLT

"I correct and discipline everyone I love."

Rev. 3:19 NLT

Temptation

....

"Watch and pray, lest you enter into temptation."

Matt. 26:41 NKJV

"Temptations are inevitable, but what sorrow awaits the person who does the tempting."

Matt. 18:7 NLT

"Pray that you may not enter into temptation."

Luke 22:46 ESV

"Lead us not into temptation, but deliver us from the evil one."

Matt. 6:13 NIV

"Worship the Lord your God, and serve Him only."

Matt. 4:10 NIV

"If they keep quiet, the stones will cry out."

Luke 19:40 NIV

"The hour is coming when you will neither on this mountain, nor in Jerusalem, worship the Father."

John 4:21 NKJV

Worship

"You worship what you do not know; we know what we worship, for salvation is of the Jews."

John 4:22 NKJV

"True worshipers will worship the Father in spirit and truth; for the Father is seeking such to worship Him."

John 4:23 NKJV

"God is spirit, and those who worship Him must worship in spirit and truth."

John 4:24 ESV

"Do not put the Lord your God to the test."

Matt. 4:7 NIV

"You shall worship the Lord your God and Him only shall you serve."

Matt. 4:10 ESV

"Let your light so shine before men, that they may see your good works and glorify your Father in heaven."

Matt. 5:16 NKJV

"You shall not murder."

Matt. 5:21 ESV

"You shall not commit adultery."

Matt. 5:27 ESV

"You shall not swear falsely, but shall perform your oaths to the Lord."

Matt. 5:33 NKJV

"If someone slaps you on the right cheek, offer the other cheek also."

Matt. 5:39 NLT

"Love your enemies and pray for those who persecute you."

Matt. 5:44 NIV

"You therefore must be perfect, as your heavenly Father is perfect."

Matt. 5:48 ESV

"When you pray, go into your room, and when you have shut your door, pray to your Father."

Matt. 6:6 NKJV

"Do to others what you would have them do to you."

Matt. 7:12 NIV

"Follow Me and be My disciple."

Matt. 9:9 NLT

"Come to Me, all you who are weary and burdened."

Matt. 11:28 NIV

"What God has joined together, let no one separate."

Matt. 19:6 NIV

"You shall not murder, you shall not commit adultery, you shall not steal, you shall not give false testimony, honor your father and mother, and love your neighbor as yourself."

Matt. 19:18-19 NIV

"Give to God what belongs to God."

Matt. 22:21 NLT

"Love your neighbor as yourself."

Matt. 22:39 NKJV

"Make disciples of all the nations, baptizing them in the name of the Father and of the Son and of the Holy Spirit."

Matt. 28:19 NKJV

"Love the Lord your God with all your heart and with all your soul and with all your mind and with all your strength."

Mark 12:30 NIV

Jesus' Commands to His Followers

"Go into all the world and proclaim the gospel to the whole creation."

Mark 16:15 ESV

"Follow Me."

Luke 5:27 NKJV

"Love your enemies, do good, and lend, hoping for nothing in return; and your reward will be great."

Luke 6:35 NKJV

"Be merciful, just as your Father also is merciful."

Luke 6:36 NKJV

"Judge not, and you will not be judged; condemn not, and you will not be condemned; forgive, and you will be forgiven."

Luke 6:37 ESV

"Go and preach the kingdom of God."

Luke 9:60 NKJV

"Seek the kingdom of God."

Luke 12:31 NKJV

"Sin no more."

John 5:14 ESV

Jesus' Commands to His Followers

....

"Do not work for food that spoils, but for food that endures to eternal life."

John 6:27 NIV

"This is the work of God, that you believe in Him whom He has sent."

John 6:29 ESV

"Do not judge by appearances, but judge with right judgment."

John 7:24 ESV

"Believe in the light while you have the light, so that you may become children of light."

John 12:36 NIV

"I have set you an example that you should do as I have done for you."

John 13:15 NIV

"Trust in God, and trust also in Me."

John 14:1 NLT

"If you love Me, keep My commandments."

John 14:15 NKJV

"Whoever has My commands and keeps them is the one who loves Me."

John 14:21 NIV

"If you keep My commandments, you will abide in My love."

John 15:10 ESV

"You are My friends if you do whatever I command you."

John 15:14 NKJV

"This is My command: Love each other."

John 15:17 NLT

JESUS' WORDS ABOUT SALVATION AND ETERNAL LIFE

Salvation

"He who endures to the end will be saved."

Matt. 10:22 NKJV

"When they see what I do, they will learn nothing.
When they hear what I say, they will not understand.
Otherwise, they will turn to Me and be forgiven."

Mark 4:12 NLT

"The Son of Man did not come to be served, but to serve, and to give His life a ransom for many."

Mark 10:45 NKJV

"Anyone who believes and is baptized will be saved."

Mark 16:16 NLT

"Your faith has saved you."

Luke 7:50 ESV

"Today salvation has come to this house."

Luke 19:9 NKJV

"The Son of Man came to seek and to save the lost."

Luke 19:10 NIV

Salvation

"God so loved the world that He gave His only begotten Son, that whoever believes in Him should not perish but have everlasting life. For God did not send His Son into the world to condemn the world, but that the world through Him might be saved."

John 3:16-17 NKJV

"Straighten up and raise your heads, because your redemption is drawing near."

Luke 21:28 ESV

"You must be born again."

John 3:7 ESV

"You will know the truth, and the truth will set you free."

John 8:32 ESV

"Whoever believes in Him is not condemned, but whoever does not believe is condemned already, because He has not believed in the name of the only Son of God."

John 3:18 ESV

"I am the gate; whoever enters through Me will be saved."

John 10:9 NIV

Eternal Life

"The gate is narrow and the way that is hard that leads to life, and those who find it are few."

Matt. 7:14 ESV

"If you give up your life for Me, you will find it."

Matt. 10:39 NLT

"If you try to hang on to your life, you will lose it. But if you give up your life for My sake, you will save it."

Matt. 16:25 NLT

"Whoever hears My word and believes Him who sent Me has eternal life."

John 5:24 ESV

"Some who are standing here will not taste death before they see the Son of Man coming in His kingdom."

Matt. 16:28 NIV

"Everyone who has given up houses or brothers or sisters or father or mother or children or property, for My sake, will receive a hundred times as much in return and will inherit eternal life."

Matt. 19:29 NLT

"Come, you who are blessed by My Father; take your inheritance, the kingdom prepared for you since the creation of the world."

Matt. 25:34 NIV

Eternal Life

"Whoever wants to save their life will lose it, but whoever loses their life for Me will save it."

Luke 9:24 NIV

"I am with you always, to the end of the age."

Matt. 28:20 ESV

"Stand firm, and you will win life."

Luke 21:19 NIV

"That which is born of the flesh is flesh, and that which is born of the Spirit is spirit."

John 3:6 NKJV

"Anyone who believes in God's Son has eternal life."

John 3:36 NLT

"The Son of Man must be lifted up, that everyone who believes may have eternal life in Him."

John 3:14-15 NIV

"You search the Scriptures, for in them you think you have eternal life; and these are they which testify of Me. But you are not willing to come to Me that you may have life."

John 5:39-40 NKJV

Eternal Life

"My Father's will is that everyone who looks to the Son and believes in Him shall have eternal life."

John 6:40 NIV

"The Spirit alone gives eternal life. Human effort accomplishes nothing. And the very words I have spoken to you are spirit and life."

John 6:63 NLT

"I am the resurrection and the life. Anyone who believes in Me will live, even after dying."

John 11:25 NLT

"This is eternal life: that they know You, the only true God, and Jesus Christ, whom You have sent."

John 17:3 NIV

"I am the living One. I died, but look – I am alive forever and ever! And I hold the keys of death and the grave."

Rev. 1:18 NLT

"All the dead in their graves will hear the voice of God's Son, and they will rise again. Those who have done good will rise to experience eternal life, and those who have continued in evil will rise to experience judgment."

John 5:28-29 NLT

Sin

"Everyone who looks at a woman with lustful intent has already committed adultery with her in his heart."

Matt. 5:28 ESV

"Out of the heart come evil thoughts – murder, adultery, sexual immorality, theft, false testimony, slander."

Matt. 15:19 NIV

"If your hand or foot causes you to sin, cut it off."

Matt. 18:8 NKJV

"If your eye causes you to sin, tear it out and throw it away."

Matt. 18:9 NKJV

"If you hold anything against anyone, forgive them, so that your Father in heaven may forgive you your sins."

Mark 11:25 NKJV

"Your sins are forgiven."

Luke 7:48 NKJV

"If another believer sins, rebuke that person; then if there is repentance, forgive."

Luke 17:3 NLT

"The world's sin is that it refuses to believe in Me."

John 16:9 ESV

Repentance

"Repent of your sins and turn to God."

Matt. 4:17 NLT

"Repent, and believe in the gospel."

Mark 1:15 NKJV

"There is forgiveness of sins for all who repent."

Luke 24:47 NLT

"There will be more joy in heaven over one sinner who repents than over ninety-nine righteous persons who need no repentance."

Luke 15:7 ESV

"There is joy in the presence of God's angels when even one sinner repents."

Luke 15:10 NLT

"Open their eyes, so that they may turn from darkness to light and from the power of Satan to God."

Acts 26:18 NKJV

"Remember therefore from where you have fallen; repent, and do the works you did at first."

Rev. 2:5 ESV

"Repent, or else I will come to you quickly and will fight against them with the sword of My mouth."

Rev. 2:16 NKJV

"Remember therefore how you have received and heard; hold fast and repent."

Rev. 3:3 NKJV

"Be zealous and repent."

Rev. 3:19 NKJV

"God so loved the world that He gave His only begotten Son, that whoever believes in Him should not perish but have everlasting life."

John 3:16 NKJV

"Go home to your friends and tell them how much the Lord has done for you, and how He has had mercy on you."

Mark 5:19 ESV

"Be merciful, just as your Father also is merciful."

Luke 6:36 NKJV

God's Love

"As the Father loved Me, I also have loved you."

John 15:9 NKJV

"If you keep My commandments, you will abide in My love, just as I have kept My Father's commandments and abide in His love. These things I have spoken to you, that My joy may be in you, and that your joy may be full."

John 15:10-11 ESV

"The Father Himself loves you, because you have loved Me."

John 16:27 NKJV

"I correct and discipline everyone I love."

Rev. 3:19 NLT

"If God cares so wonderfully for wildflowers that are here today and thrown into the fire tomorrow, He will certainly care for you."

Matt. 6:30 NLT

God's Forgiveness

"Be encouraged, My child! Your sins are forgiven."

Matt. 9:2 NLT

"If a man has a hundred sheep, and one of them has gone astray, does he not leave the ninety-nine on the mountains and go in search of the one that went astray? And if he finds it, truly, I say to you, he rejoices over it more than over the ninety-nine that never went astray. So it is not the will of My Father who is in heaven that one of these little ones should perish."

Matt. 18:12–14 ESV

"This is My blood of the covenant, which is poured out for many for the forgiveness of sins."

Matt. 26:28 ESV

"Truly I tell you, people can be forgiven all their sins."

Mark 3:28 NLT

"There is joy in the presence of the angels of God over one sinner who repents."

Luke 15:10 NKJV

"If you forgive those who sin against you, your heavenly Father will forgive you."

Matt. 6:14 NLT

"There is forgiveness of sins for all who repent."

Luke 24:47 NLT

"They will receive forgiveness for their sins and be given a place among God's people, who are set apart by faith in Me."

Acts 26:18 NLT

JESUS' WORDS ON THE WORD OF GOD AND PRAYER

"People do not live by bread alone, but by every word that comes from the mouth of God."

Matt. 4:4 NLT

"Not even the smallest detail of God's law will disappear until its purpose is achieved."

Matt. 5:18 NLT

"Your mistake is that you don't know the Scriptures, and you don't know the power of God."

Matt. 22:29 NLT

"My mother and My brothers are all those who hear God's word and obey it."

Luke 8:21 NLT

"Whoever has ears to hear, let them hear."

Mark 4:9 NIV

"Blessed rather are those who hear the word of God and obey it."

Luke 11:28 NIV

The Word of God

. . . .

"Heaven and earth will disappear, but My words will never disappear."

Luke 21:33 NLT

"It is easier for heaven and earth to disappear than for the smallest point of God's law to be overturned."

Luke 16:17 NLT

"Whoever hears My word and believes Him who sent Me has eternal life and will not be judged."

John 5:24 NIV

"The words that I have spoken to you are spirit and life."

John 6:63 ESV

"Sanctify them by Your truth. Your word is truth."

John 17:17 NKJV

"The gospel must first be preached to all nations."

Mark 13:10 NIV

"The Son of Man will go just as it is written about Him."

Mark 14:21 NIV

The Word of God

"The Good News about the Kingdom will be preached throughout the whole world."

Matt. 24:14 NLT

"Repent and believe in the gospel."

Mark 1:15 ESV

"Whoever loses their life for Me and for the gospel will save it."

Mark 8:35 NIV

"You are already clean because of the word which I have spoken to you."

John 15:3 NKJV

"If you believe, you will receive whatever you ask for in prayer."

Matt. 21:22 NIV

"Love your enemies and pray for those who persecute you."

Matt. 5:44 ESV

"When you pray, go into your room, close the door and pray to your Father, who is unseen. Then your Father, who sees what is done in secret, will reward you."

Matt. 6:6 NIV

Prayer

....

"And when you pray, do not keep on babbling like pagans, for they think they will be heard because of their many words."
Matt. 6:7 NIV

"Your Father knows what you need before you ask Him."
Matt. 6:8 ESV

"My house will be called a house of prayer."
Matt. 21:13 NIV

"Our Father in heaven,
Hallowed be Your name.
Your kingdom come.
Your will be done
On earth as it is in heaven.
Give us this day our daily bread.
And forgive us our debts,
As we forgive our debtors.
And do not lead us into temptation,
But deliver us from the Evil One.
For Yours is the kingdom and the power and the glory forever.
Amen."

Matt. 6:9-13 NKJV

Prayer

"Ask, and it will be given to you; seek, and you will find; knock, and it will be opened to you."

Matt. 7:7 NKJV

"Which one of you, if his son asks him for bread, will give him a stone? Or if he asks for a fish, will give him a serpent? If you then, who are evil, know how to give good gifts to your children, how much more will your Father who is in heaven give good things to those who ask Him!"

Matt. 7:9-11 ESV

"Pray the Lord of the harvest to send out laborers into His harvest."

Matt. 9:38 NKJV

"If two of you agree here on earth concerning anything you ask, My Father in heaven will do it for you."

Matt. 18:19 NLT

"Where two or three are gathered in My name, there am I among them."

Matt. 18:20 ESV

Prayer

....

"Whenever you stand praying, if you have anything against anyone, forgive him."

Mark 11:25 NKJV

"I want Your will to be done, not Mine."

Mark 14:36 NLT

"Bless those who curse you. Pray for those who hurt you."

Luke 6:28 NLT

"Keep watch and pray, so that you will not give in to temptation. For the spirit is willing, but the body is weak."

Matt. 26:41 NLT

"When you pray, you must not be like the hypocrites. For they love to stand and pray in the synagogues and at the street corners, that they may be seen by others."

Matt. 6:5 ESV

"This, then, is how you should pray: 'Our Father in heaven, hallowed be Your name.'"

Matt. 6:9 NIV

Prayer:

....

"Which of you shall have a friend, and go to him at midnight and say to him, 'Friend, lend me three loaves; for a friend of mine has come to me on his journey, and I have nothing to set before him'; and he will answer from within and say, 'Do not trouble me; the door is now shut, and my children are with me in bed; I cannot rise and give to you'? I say to you, though he will not rise and give to him because he is his friend, yet because of his persistence he will rise and give him as many as he needs."

Luke 11:5-8 NKJV

"Keep on asking, and you will receive what you ask for. Keep on seeking, and you will find. Keep on knocking, and the door will be opened to you."

Luke 11:9 NLT

"Which of you fathers, if your son asks for a fish, will give him a snake instead? Or if he asks for an egg, will give him a scorpion? If you then, though you are evil, know how to give good gifts to your children, how much more will your Father in heaven give the Holy Spirit to those who ask Him!"

Luke 11:11-13 NIV

Prayer

....

"Two men went up into the temple to pray, one a Pharisee and the other a tax collector. The Pharisee, standing by himself, prayed thus: 'God, I thank You that I am not like other men, extortioners, unjust, adulterers, or even like this tax collector. I fast twice a week; I give tithes of all that I get.' But the tax collector, standing far off, would not even lift up his eyes to heaven, but beat his breast, saying, 'God, be merciful to me, a sinner!' I tell you, this man went down to his house justified, rather than the other."

Luke 18:10-14 ESV

"Be always on the watch, and pray that you may be able to escape all that is about to happen, and that you may be able to stand before the Son of Man."

Luke 21:36 NIV

"Pray that you may not enter into temptation."

Luke 22:40 NKJV

"Whatever you ask in My name, that I will do, that the Father may be glorified in the Son."

John 14:13 NKJV

Prayer

....

"You may ask Me for anything in My name, and I will do it."

John 14:14 NIV

"Whatever you ask the Father in My name He may give you."

John 15:16 NKJV

"You will ask in My name, and I do not say to you that I will ask the Father on your behalf; for the Father Himself loves you, because you have loved Me and have believed that I came from God."

John 16:26-27 ESV

"I praise You, Father, Lord of heaven and earth, because You have hidden these things from the wise and learned, and revealed them to little children. Yes, Father, for this is what You were pleased to do."

Matt. 11:25-26 NIV

"My Father! If it is possible, let this cup of suffering be taken away from Me."

Matt. 26:39 NLT

"My Father, if this cannot pass unless I drink it, Your will be done."

Matt. 26:42 ESV

Prayers of Jesus

....

"I have prayed for you that your faith may not fail."

Luke 22:32 ESV

"Father, I thank You that You have heard Me. And I know that You always hear Me."

John 11:41-42 NKJV

"Father, the hour has come. Glorify Your Son, that Your Son also may glorify You, as You have given Him authority over all flesh, that He should give eternal life to as many as You have given Him.

John 17:1-2 NKJV

"My prayer is not for the world, but for those You have given Me, because they belong to You."

John 17:9 NLT

"Holy Father, keep through Your name those whom You have given Me."

John 17:11 NKJV

"I am praying not only for these disciples but also for all who will ever believe in Me through their message. I pray that they will all be one, just as You and I are one."

John 17:20-21 NLT

JESUS' PROMISES AND BLESSINGS

"Anyone who obeys God's laws and teaches them will be called great in the Kingdom of Heaven."

Matt. 5:19 NLT

"Seek the Kingdom of God above all else, and live righteously, and He will give you everything you need."

Matt. 6:33 NLT

"The one who endures to the end will be saved."

Matt. 10:22 ESV

"Come to Me, all you who are weary and burdened, and I will give you rest."

Matt. 11:28 NIV

"Whoever speaks a word against the Son of Man will be forgiven."

Matt. 12:32 ESV

"I will give you the keys of the kingdom of heaven."

Matt. 16:19 ESV

"The Son of Man will come in the glory of His Father with His angels, and then He will reward each according to his works."

Matt. 16:27 NKJV

"Where two or three are gathered together in My name, I am there in the midst of them."

Matt. 18:20 NKJV

"In the new world, when the Son of Man will sit on His glorious throne, you who have followed Me will also sit on twelve thrones."

Matt. 19:28 ESV

Jesus' Promises

"I will not drink of this fruit of the vine from now on until that day when I drink it new with you in My Father's kingdom."

Matt. 26:29 NKJV

"I am with you always, even to the end of the age."

Matt. 28:20 NLT

"I assure you that everyone who has given up house or brothers or sisters or mother or father or children or property, for My sake and for the Good News, will receive now in return a hundred times as many houses, sisters, brothers, mothers, children, and property."

Mark 10:29-30 NLT

"Whoever publicly acknowledges Me before others, the Son of Man will also acknowledge before the angels of God."

Luke 12:8 NIV

"You shall see heaven open, and the angels of God ascending and descending upon the Son of Man."

John 1:51 NKJV

"The time is coming when all the dead in their graves will hear the voice of God's Son."

John 5:28 NLT

"Those who have done what is good will rise to live, and those who have done what is evil will rise to be condemned."

John 5:29 NIV

"Whoever believes has eternal life."

John 6:47 ESV

"Whoever obeys My word will never see death."

John 8:51 NIV

"Whoever eats My flesh and drinks My blood has eternal life, and I will raise him up at the last day."

John 6:54 NKJV

"Everyone who lives in Me and believes in Me will never ever die."

John 11:26 NLT

"When I am lifted up from the earth, will draw all people to Myself."

John 12:32 ESV

"If you know these things, blessed are you if you do them."

John 13:17 NKJV

"I will come back and take you to be with Me that you also may be where I am."

John 14:3 NIV

Jesus' Promises

"Whatever you ask in My name, that I will do."

John 14:13 NKJV

"I will not leave you as orphans; I will come to you."

John 14:18 ESV

"The one who loves Me will be loved by My Father, and I too will love them and show Myself to them."

John 14:21 NIV

"If you abide in Me, and My words abide in you, ask whatever you wish, and it will be done for you."

John 15:7 ESV

"Whatever you ask the Father in My name He will give you."

John 16:23 NKJV

"My grace is sufficient for you, for My strength is made perfect in weakness."

2 Cor. 12:9 NKJV

"It is done! I am the Alpha and the Omega, the Beginning and the End. I will give of the fountain of the water of life freely to him who thirsts."

Rev. 21:6 NKJV

Jesus' Blessings

"Blessed are the poor in spirit, for theirs is the kingdom of heaven."

Matt. 5:3 NIV

"Blessed are those who mourn, for they will be comforted."

Matt. 5:4 NIV

"Blessed are the meek, for they will inherit the earth."

Matt. 5:5 NIV

"Blessed are those who hunger and thirst for righteousness, for they will be filled."

Matt. 5:6 NIV

"Blessed are the merciful, for they will be shown mercy."

Matt. 5:7 NIV

"Blessed are the pure in heart, for they will see God."

Matt. 5:8 NIV

"Blessed are the peacemakers, for they will be called children of God."

Matt. 5:9 NIV

"Blessed are those who are persecuted because of righteousness, for theirs is the kingdom of heaven."

Matt. 5:10 NIV

Jesus' Blessings

"Blessed are you when people insult you, persecute you and falsely say all kinds of evil against you because of Me."

Matt. 5:11 NIV

"Blessed is he who comes in the name of the Lord."

Matt. 23:39 ESV

"Blessed are you who are hungry now, for you shall be satisfied. Blessed are you who weep now, for you shall laugh."

Luke 6:21 ESV

"Blessed is anyone who does not stumble on account of Me."

Luke 7:23 NIV

"Blessed are the eyes that see what you see!"

Luke 10:23 ESV

"Blessed rather are those who hear the word of God and obey it."

Luke 11:28 NIV

"You will be blessed."

Luke 14:14 NKJV

"If you know these things, blessed are you if you do them."

John 13:17 NKJV

Jesus' Blessings

"Holy Father, protect them by the power of Your name, the name You gave Me, so that they may be one as We are one."

John 17:11 NIV

"My prayer is not that You take them out of the world but that You protect them from the evil one."

John 17:15 NIV

"I pray that they will all be one, just as You and I are one — as You are in Me, Father, and I am in You."

John 17:21 NLT

"Blessed are those who have not seen and yet have believed."

John 20:29 ESV

"May they experience such perfect unity that the world will know that You sent Me and that You love them as much as You love Me."

John 17:23 NLT

"Peace be with you."

John 20:19 ESV

"Receive the Holy Spirit."

John 20:22 ESV

"Blessed are all who are watching for Me."

Rev. 16:15 NLT

"Blessed are those who obey the words of prophecy."

Rev. 22:7 NLT

"Blessed are those who wash their robes, so that they may have the right to the tree of life and that they may enter the city by the gates."

Rev. 22:14 ESV

"Blessed are you who are poor, for yours is the kingdom of God.
Blessed are you who are hungry now, for you shall be satisfied.
Blessed are you who weep now, for you shall laugh.
Blessed are you when people hate you and when they
exclude you and revile you and spurn your name as evil,
on account of the Son of Man!"

Luke 6:20-22 ESV

Beatitudes

....

"Blessed are the poor in spirit,
for theirs is the kingdom of heaven.
Blessed are those who mourn,
for they will be comforted.
Blessed are the meek,
for they will inherit the earth.
Blessed are those who hunger and thirst for righteousness,
for they will be filled.
Blessed are the merciful,
for they will be shown mercy.

Blessed are the pure in heart,
for they will see God.
Blessed are the peacemakers,
for they will be called children of God.
Blessed are those who are persecuted because of righteousness,
for theirs is the kingdom of heaven.
Blessed are you when people insult you, persecute you and
falsely say all kinds of evil against you because of Me."

Matt. 5:3-11 NIV

JESUS' WORDS
ON HIS DEATH,
RESURRECTION AND
THE SECOND COMING

"The Son of Man is going to be delivered into the hands of men. They will kill Him, and after three days He will rise."

Mark 9:31 NIV

"The Son of Man will be three days and three nights in the heart of the earth."

Matt. 12:40 NIV

"The Son of Man will be handed over to be crucified."

Matt. 26:2 NLT

....

"I am the resurrection and the life. The one who believes in Me will live, even though they die."

John 11:25 NIV

"The Son of Man must suffer many things and be rejected by the elders and chief priests and scribes, and be killed, and on the third day be raised."

Luke 9:22 ESV

"Everything written about Me by the prophets will come true."

Luke 22:37 NLT

"My time has not yet come."

John 2:4 NLT

"A man planted a vineyard. He put a wall around it, dug a pit for the winepress and built a watchtower. Then he rented the vineyard to some farmers and moved to another place. At harvest time he sent a servant to the tenants to collect from them some of the fruit of the vineyard. But they seized him, beat him and sent him away empty-handed. Then he sent another servant to them; they struck this man on the head and treated him shamefully. He sent still another, and that one they killed. He sent many others; some of them they beat, others they killed. He had one left to send, a son, whom he loved. He sent him last of all, saying, 'They will respect my son.' But the tenants said to one another, 'This is the heir. Come, let's kill him, and

His Death

....

the inheritance will be ours.' So they took him and killed him, and threw him out of the vineyard. What then will the owner of the vineyard do? He will come and kill those tenants and give the vineyard to others."

Mark 12:1-9 NIV

"The Son of Man will be betrayed to the chief priests and to the scribes; and they will condemn Him to death and deliver Him to the Gentiles; and they will mock Him, and scourge Him, and spit on Him, and kill Him."

Mark 10:33-34 NKJV

"The hour has come for the Son of Man to be glorified."

John 12:23 NIV

"I will be with you only a little longer. Then I will return to the one who sent Me."

John 7:33 NLT

"I am going away, and you will look for Me, and you will die in your sin."

John 8:21 NIV

His Death

"The time for judging this world has come, when Satan, the ruler of this world, will be cast out."

John 12:31 NLT

"My light will shine for you just a little longer. Walk in the light while you can, so the darkness will not overtake you."

John 12:35 NLT

"A little while longer and the world will see Me no more."

John 14:19 NKJV

"I go to the Father, and you will see Me no more."

John 16:10 NLT

"I came from the Father and have come into the world, and now I am leaving the world and going to the Father."

John 16:28 ESV

"This is My body which is broken for you."

1 Cor. 11:24 NKJV

"The Messiah will suffer and rise from the dead on the third day."

Luke 24:46 NIV

The Seven Words of Jesus on the Cross

1. "Father, forgive them, for they do not know what they do."
   Luke 23:34 NKJV

2. "Truly, I say to you, today you will be with Me in Paradise."
   Luke 23:43 ESV

3. "Woman, behold your Son!" Then He said to the disciple,
   "Behold your mother!"
   John 19:26-27 NKJV

4. "My God, My God, why have You forsaken Me?"

Mark 15:34 ESV

5. "I thirst."

John 19:28 NLT

6. "It is finished!"

John 19:30 NKJV

7. "Father, into Your hands I commit My spirit."

Luke 23:46 NIV

"Don't tell anyone what you have seen, until the Son of Man has been raised from the dead."

Matt. 17:9 NIV

"At the resurrection people will neither marry nor be given in marriage; they will be like the angels in heaven."

Matt. 22:30 NIV

"It is written, that the Christ should suffer and on the third day rise from the dead."

Luke 24:46 ESV

"Destroy this temple, and in three days I will raise it up."

John 2:19 NKJV

"I am the resurrection and the life."

John 11:25 NKJV

"After I am raised from the dead, I will go ahead of you to Galilee and meet you there."

Mark 14:28 NLT

"As Moses lifted up the serpent in the wilderness, so must the Son of Man be lifted up, that whoever believes in Him may have eternal life."

John 3:14-15 ESV

The Second Coming

"The kingdom of heaven is like a king who prepared a wedding banquet for his son. He sent his servants to those who had been invited to the banquet to tell them to come, but they refused to come. Then he sent some more servants and said, 'Tell those who have been invited that I have prepared my dinner: My oxen and fattened cattle have been butchered, and everything is ready. Come to the wedding banquet.' But they paid no attention and went off – one to his field, another to his business. The rest seized his servants, mistreated them and killed them. The king was enraged. He sent his army and destroyed those murderers and burned their city. Then he said to his servants, 'The wedding banquet is ready, but those I invited did not deserve to come. So go to the street corners and invite anyone you find."

Matt. 22:2-14 NIV

"The sun will be darkened, and the moon will not give its light; the stars will fall from heaven, and the powers of the heavens will be shaken. Then the sign of the Son of Man will appear in heaven, and then all the tribes of the earth will mourn, and they will see the Son of Man coming on the clouds of heaven with power and great glory."

Matt. 24:29-30 NKJV

"He will send His angels with a great sound of a trumpet, and they will gather together His elect from the four winds, from one end of heaven to the other."

Matt. 24:31 NKJV

The Second Coming

"Concerning that day and hour no one knows, not even the angels of heaven, nor the Son, but the Father only."

Matt. 24:36 ESV

"As it was in the days of Noah, so it will be at the coming of the Son of Man. For in the days before the flood, people were eating and drinking, marrying and giving in marriage, up to the day Noah entered the ark; and they knew nothing about what would happen until the flood came and took them all away. That is how it will be at the coming of the Son of Man. Two men will be in the field; one will be taken and the other left. Two women will be grinding with a hand mill; one will be taken and the other left."

Matt. 24:37-41 NIV

"Keep watch, because you do not know on what day your Lord will come."

Matt. 24:42 NIV

"At that time the kingdom of heaven will be like ten virgins who took their lamps and went out to meet the bridegroom. Five of them were foolish and five were wise. The foolish ones took their lamps but did not take any oil with them. The wise ones, however, took oil in jars along with their lamps. The bridegroom was a long time in coming, and they all became drowsy and fell asleep. At midnight the cry rang out: 'Here's the bridegroom! Come out to meet him!' Then all the virgins woke up and trimmed their lamps. The foolish ones said to the wise,

The Second Coming

'Give us some of your oil; our lamps are going out.' 'No,' they replied, 'there may not be enough for both us and you. Instead, go to those who sell oil and buy some for yourselves.' But while they were on their way to buy the oil, the bridegroom arrived. The virgins who were ready went in with him to the wedding banquet. And the door was shut. Later the others also came. 'Lord, Lord,' they said, 'open the door for us!' But he replied, 'Truly I tell you, I don't know you.' Therefore keep watch, because you do not know the day or the hour."

Matt. 25:1-13 NIV

"When the Son of Man comes in His glory, and all the angels with Him, then He will sit upon His glorious throne."

Matt. 25:31 NLT

"You will see the Son of Man seated in the place of power at God's right hand and coming on the clouds of heaven."

Matt. 26:64 NLT

The Second Coming

"I am going away, but I will come back to you again. If you really loved Me, you would be happy that I am going to the Father, who is greater than I am."

John 14:28 NLT

"The sun will be darkened, and the moon will not give its light, and the stars will be falling from heaven, and the powers in the heavens will be shaken. And then they will see the Son of Man coming in clouds with great power and glory. And then He will send out the angels and gather His elect from the four winds, from the ends of the earth to the ends of heaven."

Mark 13:24-27 ESV

"The coming of the Son of Man can be illustrated by the story of a man going on a long trip. When he left home, he gave each of his slaves instructions about the work they were to do, and he told the gatekeeper to watch for his return. You, too, must keep watch! For you don't know when the master of the household will return – in the evening, at midnight, before dawn, or at daybreak. Don't let him find you sleeping when he arrives without warning. I say to you what I say to everyone: Watch for him!"

Mark 13:34-37 NLT

"Repent of your sins and turn to God, for the Kingdom of Heaven is near."

Matt. 3:2 NLT

"Whoever is ashamed of Me and My words, the Son of Man will be ashamed of them when He comes in His glory and in the glory of the Father and of the holy angels."

Luke 9:26 NIV

"Be dressed ready for service and keep your lamps burning, like servants waiting for their master to return from a wedding banquet, so that when he comes and knocks they can immediately open the door for him. It will be good for those servants whose master finds them watching when he comes. Truly I tell you, he will dress himself to serve, will have them recline at the table and will come and wait on them. It will be good for those servants whose master finds them ready, even if he comes in the middle of the night or toward daybreak. But understand this: If the owner of the house had known at what hour the thief was coming, he would not have let his house be broken into."

Luke 12:35-39 NIV

The Second Coming

"The Son of Man is coming at an hour you do not expect."

Luke 12:40 NKJV

"There will be signs in the sun, in the moon, and in the stars; and on the earth distress of nations, with perplexity, the sea and the waves roaring; men's hearts failing them from fear and the expectation of those things which are coming on the earth, for the powers of the heavens will be shaken."

Luke 21:25-26 NKJV

"Everyone will see the Son of Man coming on a cloud with power and great glory."

Luke 21:27 NLT

"I will come as unexpectedly as a thief!"

Rev. 16:15 NLT

"I am coming soon! My reward is with Me, and I will give to each person according to what they have done."

Rev. 22:12 NIV

JESUS' WORDS ON THE KINGDOM OF HEAVEN AND THE KINGDOM OF GOD

"The Kingdom of Heaven is near."

Matt. 4:17 NLT

"Unless your righteousness is better than the righteousness of the teachers of religious law and the Pharisees, you will never enter the Kingdom of Heaven!"

Matt. 5:20 NLT

"Many will come from east and west, and sit down with Abraham, Isaac, and Jacob in the kingdom of heaven."

Matt. 8:11 NKJV

The Kingdom of Heaven

"The Kingdom of Heaven is like a farmer who planted good seed in his field."

Matt. 13:24 NLT

"The Kingdom of Heaven is like a mustard seed planted in a field."

Matt. 13:31 NLT

"The Kingdom of heaven is like treasure hidden in a field. When a man found it, he hid it again, and then in his joy went and sold all he had and bought that field."

Matt. 13:44 NIV

"The kingdom of heaven is like a merchant in search of fine pearls."

Matt. 13:45 ESV

"The kingdom of heaven is like a net that was thrown into the sea and gathered fish of every kind."

Matt. 13:47 ESV

"Unless you are converted and become as little children, you will by no means enter the kingdom of heaven."

Matt. 18:3 NKJV

The Kingdom of Heaven

"The Kingdom of heaven is like a king who wanted to settle accounts with his servants."

Matt. 18:23 NIV

"Let the children come to Me. Don't stop them! For the Kingdom of Heaven belongs to those who are like these children."

Matt. 19:14 NLT

"It is hard for someone who is rich to enter the kingdom of heaven."

Matt. 19:23 NIV

"The kingdom of heaven is like a master of a house who went out early in the morning to hire laborers for his vineyard."

Matt. 20:1 ESV

"The kingdom of heaven is like a king who prepared a wedding banquet for his son."

Matt. 22:2 NIV

"Not everyone who calls out to Me, 'Lord! Lord!' will enter the Kingdom of Heaven. Only those who actually do the will of My Father in heaven will enter."

Matt. 7:21 NLT

The Kingdom of God

"Seek first the kingdom of God and His righteousness."

Matt. 6:33 NKJV

"The kingdom of God will be taken from you and given to a nation bearing the fruits of it."

Matt. 21:43 NKJV

"To you it has been given to know the mystery of the kingdom of God."

Mark 4:11 NKJV

"It is easier for a camel to go through the eye of a needle than for someone who is rich to enter the kingdom of God."

Mark 10:25 NIV

"Whoever does not receive the kingdom of God like a child shall not enter it."

Mark 10:15 ESV

"How difficult it will be for those who have wealth to enter the kingdom of God!"

Mark 10:23 ESV

The Kingdom of God

"I tell you the truth, some standing here right now will not die before they see the Kingdom of God arrive in great power!"

Mark 9:1 NLT

"You are not far from the kingdom of God."

Mark 12:34 ESV

"No one who puts a hand to the plow and looks back is fit for service in the kingdom of God."

Luke 9:62 NIV

"The kingdom of God has come near."

Luke 10:11 ESV

"What is the kingdom of God like? And to what shall I compare it? It is like a mustard seed, which a man took and put in his garden; and it grew and became a large tree, and the birds of the air nested in its branches."

Luke 13:18-19 ESV

"What shall I compare the kingdom of God to? It is like yeast that a woman took and mixed into about sixty pounds of flour until it worked all through the dough."

Luke 13:20-21 NIV

The Kingdom of God

"People will come from east and west, and from north and south, and recline at table in the Kingdom of God."

Luke 13:29 ESV

"Seek the Kingdom of God above all else, and He will give you everything you need."

Luke 12:31 NLT

"The Kingdom of God is not coming with signs to be observed."

Luke 17:20 ESV

"The Kingdom of God is within you."

Luke 17:21 NKJV

"Unless you are born again, you cannot see the Kingdom of God."

John 3:3 NLT

"No one can enter the kingdom of God unless they are born of water and the Spirit."

John 3:5 NIV

"My kingdom is not of this world."

John 18:36 ESV

JESUS' WARNINGS
AND WORDS ON
THE END TIMES,
AND THE EVIL ONE

"Beware of practicing your righteousness before other people in order to be seen by them."

Matt. 6:1 ESV

"Beware of false prophets who come disguised as harmless sheep but are really vicious wolves."

Matt. 7:15 NLT

"Not everyone who calls out to Me, 'Lord! Lord!' will enter the Kingdom of Heaven. Only those who actually do the will of My Father in heaven will enter."

Matt. 7:21 NLT

Warnings

"Everyone who denies Me here on earth, I will also deny before My Father in heaven."

Matt. 10:33 NLT

"Everyone will have to give account on the day of judgment for every empty word they have spoken."

Matt. 12:36 NIV

"By your words you will be justified, and by your words you will be condemned."

Matt. 12:37 NKJV

"Those who use the sword will die by the sword."

Matt. 26:52 NLT

"Whoever blasphemes against the Holy Spirit will never be forgiven; they are guilty of an eternal sin."

Mark 3:29 NIV

"If anyone says to you, 'Look, here is the Messiah!' or, 'Look, there He is!' do not believe it."

Mark 13:21 NIV

Warnings

"False messiahs and false prophets will rise up and perform signs and wonders so as to deceive, if possible, even God's chosen ones. Watch out! I have warned you about this ahead of time!"

Mark 13:22-23 NLT

"Be on guard! Be alert! You do not know when that time will come."

Mark 13:33 NIV

"Anyone who believes and is baptized will be saved. But anyone who refuses to believe will be condemned."

Mark 16:16 NLT

"Don't let anyone mislead you, for many will come in My name, claiming, 'I am the Messiah,' and saying, 'The time has come!' But don't believe them."

Luke 21:8 NLT

"Watch yourselves lest your hearts be weighed down with dissipation and drunkenness and cares of this life, and that day come upon you suddenly like a trap."

Luke 21:34 ESV

"Be always on the watch, and pray that you may be able to escape all that is about to happen, and that you may be able to stand before the Son of Man."

Luke 21:36 NIV

"You would die in your sins; if you do not believe that I am He, you will indeed die in your sins."

John 8:24 NIV

"Judgment will come because the ruler of this world has already been judged."

John 16:11 NLT

"Many will say to Me in that day, 'Lord, Lord, have we not prophesied in Your name, cast out demons in Your name, and done many wonders in Your name?' And then I will declare to them, 'I never knew you; depart from Me, you who practice lawlessness!'"

Matt. 7:22-23 NKJV

"Brother will betray brother to death, and a father his child; children will rebel against their parents and have them put to death."

Matt. 10:21 NIV

The End Times

"The kingdom of heaven is like a man who sowed good seed in his field. But while everyone was sleeping, his enemy came and sowed weeds among the wheat, and went away. When the wheat sprouted and formed heads, then the weeds also appeared. "The owner's servants came to him and said, 'Sir, didn't you sow good seed in your field? Where then did the weeds come from?' 'An enemy did this,' he replied. The servants asked him, 'Do you want us to go and pull them up?' 'No,' he answered, 'because while you are pulling the weeds, you may uproot the wheat with them. Let both grow together until the harvest. At that time I will tell the harvesters: First collect the weeds and tie them in bundles to be burned; then gather the wheat and bring it into my barn.'"

Matt. 13:24-30 NIV

"This is how it will be at the end of the age. The angels will come and separate the wicked from the righteous."

Matt. 13:49 NIV

"Many will come in My name, saying, 'I am the Christ,' and will deceive many."

Matt. 24:5 NKJV

"The Good News about the Kingdom will be preached throughout the whole world, so that all nations will hear it; and then the end will come."

Matt. 24:14 NLT

The End Times

"False christs and false prophets will rise and show great signs and wonders to deceive, if possible, even the elect."

Matt. 24:24 NKJV

"When the Son of Man comes in His glory, and all the angels with Him, He will sit on His glorious throne. All the nations will be gathered before Him, and He will separate the people one from another as a shepherd separates the sheep from the goats. He will put the sheep on His right and the goats on His left."

Matt. 25:31-33 NIV

"The King will say to those on His right, 'Come, you who are blessed by My Father; take your inheritance, the kingdom prepared for you since the creation of the world. For I was hungry and you gave Me something to eat, I was thirsty and you gave Me something to drink, I was a stranger and you invited Me in, I needed clothes and you clothed Me, I was sick and you looked after Me, I was in prison and you came to visit Me.' "

Matt. 25:34-36 NIV

"Then He will say to those on His left, 'Depart from Me, you who are cursed, into the eternal fire prepared for the devil and his angels. For I was hungry and you gave Me nothing to eat, I was thirsty and you gave Me nothing to drink, I was a stranger and you did not invite Me in, I needed clothes and you did not clothe Me, I was sick and in prison and you did not look after Me.' "

Matt. 25:41-43 NIV

"When you hear of wars and rumors of wars, do not be alarmed. This must take place, but the end is not yet."

Mark 13:7 ESV

"The gospel must first be preached to all the nations."

Mark 13:10 NKJV

"Now learn this lesson from the fig tree: As soon as its twigs get tender and its leaves come out, you know that summer is near. Even so, when you see all these things, you know that it is near, right at the door. Truly I tell you, this generation will certainly not pass away until all these things have happened."

Matt. 24:32-34 NIV

The End Times

"The day is coming when you will see the sacrilegious object that causes desecration standing where he should not be. Then those in Judea must flee to the hills. A person out on the deck of a roof must not go down into the house to pack. A person out in the field must not return even to get a coat. How terrible it will be for pregnant women and for nursing mothers in those days. And pray that your flight will not be in winter. For there will be greater anguish in those days than at any time since God created the world. And it will never be so great again. In fact, unless the Lord shortens that time of calamity, not a single person will survive. But for the sake of His chosen ones He has shortened those days."

Mark 13:14-20 NLT

"No one knows the day or hour when these things will happen, not even the angels in heaven or the Son Himself. Only the Father knows. And since you don't know when that time will come, be on guard! Stay alert!"

Mark 13:32-33 NLT

"There is nothing hidden that will not be disclosed, and nothing concealed that will not be known or brought out into the open."

Luke 8:17 NIV

"I am with you always, even to the end of the age."

Matt. 28:20 NLT

The End Times

"The one who endures to the end will be saved."

Mark 13:13 NLT

"Nation will rise against nation, and kingdom against kingdom. And there will be great earthquakes in various places, and famines and pestilences; and there will be fearful sights and great signs from heaven."

Luke 21:10-11 NKJV

"There will be a time of great persecution."

Luke 21:12 NLT

"Let your 'Yes' be 'Yes,' and your 'No,' 'No.' For whatever is more than these is from the Evil One."

Matt. 5:37 NKJV

"Be gone, Satan!"

Matt. 4:10 ESV

"Do not lead us into temptation, but deliver us from the evil one."

Matt. 6:13 NKJV

The Evil One

....

"The thief comes only to steal and kill and destroy."

John 10:10 ESV

"If Satan casts out Satan, he is divided against himself. How then will his kingdom stand?"

Matt. 12:26 NKJV

"If I am empowered by Satan, what about your own exorcists? They cast out demons, too, so they will condemn you for what you have said. But if I am casting out demons by the Spirit of God, then the Kingdom of God has arrived among you."

Matt. 12:27-28 NLT

"Who is powerful enough to enter the house of a strong man like Satan and plunder his goods? Only someone even stronger – someone who could tie him up and then plunder his house."

Matt. 12:29 NLT

"When an evil spirit leaves a person, it goes into the desert, seeking rest but finding none. Then it says, 'I will return to the person I came from.' So it returns and finds its former home empty, swept, and in order. Then the spirit finds seven other spirits more evil than itself, and they all enter the person and live there. And so that person is worse off than before. That will be the experience of this evil generation."

Matt. 12:43-45 NLT

The Evil One

"When anyone hears the message about the kingdom and does not understand it, the Evil One comes and snatches away what was sown in their heart."

Matt. 13:19 NIV

"Get behind Me, Satan! You are an offense to Me, for you are not mindful of the things of God, but the things of men."

Matt. 16:23 NKJV

"Depart from Me, you who are cursed, into the eternal fire prepared for the devil and his angels."

Matt. 25:41 NIV

"I saw Satan fall like lightning from heaven."

Luke 10:18 NKJV

"Don't rejoice because evil spirits obey you; rejoice because your names are registered in heaven."

Luke 10:20 NLT

"Satan demanded to have you, that he might sift you like wheat, but I have prayed for you that your faith may not fail."

Luke 22:31-32 ESV

The Evil One

"You are of your father the devil, and your will is to do your father's desires. He was a murderer from the beginning, and has nothing to do with the truth, because there is no truth in him. When he lies, he speaks out of his own character, for he is a liar and the father of lies."

John 8:44 ESV

"The time for judging this world has come, when Satan, the ruler of this world, will be cast out."

John 12:31 NLT

"What sorrow awaits you who are rich, for you have your only happiness now."

Luke 6:24 NLT

"What sorrow awaits you who are fat and prosperous now, for a time of awful hunger awaits you. What sorrow awaits you who laugh now, for your laughing will turn to mourning and sorrow."

Luke 6:25 NLT

"What sorrow awaits you who are praised by the crowds, for their ancestors also praised false prophets."

Luke 6:26 NLT

QUESTIONS AND ANSWERS WITH JESUS

Q: "Are You the Messiah we've been expecting, or should we keep looking for someone else?"

A: "The blind see, the lame walk, the lepers are cured, the deaf hear, the dead are raised to life, and the Good News is being preached to the poor."

Matt. 11:3, 5 NLT

Q: "Why do You speak to the people in parables?"

A: "Because the knowledge of the secrets of the kingdom of heaven has been given to you, but not to them."

Matt. 13:10-11 NIV

Questions from His Disciples

Q: "Explain to us the parable that says people aren't defiled by what they eat."

A: "Anything you eat passes through the stomach and then goes into the sewer. But the words you speak come from the heart – that's what defiles you."

Matt. 15:15, 17-18 NLT

Q: "Why then do the teachers of the law say that Elijah must come first?"

A: "To be sure, Elijah comes and will restore all things. But I tell you, Elijah has already come, and they did not recognize him, but have done to him everything they wished."

Matt. 17:10-12 NIV

Q: "Who, then, is the greatest in the kingdom of heaven?"

A: "Whoever takes the lowly position of this child is the greatest in the kingdom of heaven."

Matt. 18:1, 4 NIV

Q: "Lord, how often shall my brother sin against me, and I forgive him? Up to seven times?"

A: "I do not say to you, up to seven times, but up to seventy times seven."

Matt. 18:21-22 NKJV

Questions from His Disciples

Q: "Who then can be saved?"

A: "With man this is impossible, but with God all things are possible."

Matt. 19:25-26 ESV

Q: "We have left everything and followed You. What then will we have?"

A: "In the new world, when the Son of Man will sit on His glorious throne, you who have followed Me will also sit on twelve thrones."

Matt. 19:27-28 ESV

Q: "When will these things be, and what will be the sign of Your coming and of the close of the age?"

A: "Concerning that day and hour no one knows, not even the angels of heaven, nor the Son, but the Father only."

Matt. 24:3, 36 ESV

Q: "We want to perform God's works, too. What should we do?"

A: "Believe in the One He has sent."

John 6:28-29 NLT

Questions from His Disciples

Q: "Rabbi, lately the Jews sought to stone You, and are You going there again?"

A: "Are there not twelve hours in the day? If anyone walks in the day, he does not stumble, because he sees the light of this world. But if one walks in the night, he stumbles, because the light is not in him."

John 11:8-10 NKJV

Q: "Lord, where are You going?"

A: "Where I am going you cannot follow Me now, but you shall follow Me afterward."

John 13:36 NKJV

Q: "Lord, we do not know where You are going, and how can we know the way?"

A: "I am the way, the truth, and the life. No one comes to the Father except through Me."

John 14:5-6 NKJV

Q: "Lord, show us the Father, and it is sufficient for us."

A: "Have I been with you so long, and yet you have not known Me?"

John 14:8-9 NKJV

Questions from His Disciples

Q: "Lord, why do You intend to show Yourself to us and not to the world?"

A: "Anyone who loves Me will obey My teaching. My Father will love them, and We will come to them and make Our home with them."

John 14:22-23 NIV

Q: "Is it lawful to heal on the Sabbath?"

A: "Which one of you who has a sheep, if it falls into a pit on the Sabbath, will not take hold of it and lift it out? Of how much more value is a man than a sheep! So it is lawful to do good on the Sabbath."

Matt. 12:10-12 ESV

Q: "Why do Your disciples break the tradition of the elders? For they do not wash their hands when they eat?"

A: "Why do you break the commandment of God for the sake of your tradition?"

Matt. 15:2-3 ESV

Q: "Is it lawful to divorce one's wife for any cause?"

A: "Have you not read that He who created them from the beginning made them male and female, and said, 'Therefore a man shall leave his father and his mother and hold fast to his wife, and the two shall become one flesh'? So they are no longer two but one flesh. What therefore God has joined together, let not man separate."

Matt. 19:3-6 ESV

Q: "Why then did Moses command one to give a certificate of divorce and to send her away?"

A: "Because of your hardness of heart Moses allowed you to divorce your wives, but from the beginning it was not so. And I say to you: whoever divorces his wife, except for sexual immorality, and marries another, commits adultery."

Matt. 19:7-9 ESV

Q: "Teacher, which is the great commandment in the Law?"

A: "You shall love the Lord your God with all your heart and with all your soul and with all your mind. This is the great and first commandment."

Matt. 22:36-38 ESV

Q: "Why do they do what is not lawful on the Sabbath?"

A: "The Sabbath was made for man, and not man for the Sabbath."

Mark 2:24, 27 NKJV

Q: "Are You the Christ, the Son of the Blessed?"

A: "I am. And you will see the Son of Man sitting at the right hand of the Power, and coming with the clouds of heaven."

Mark 14:61-62 NKJV

Q: "When will the Kingdom of God come?"
A: "The Kingdom of God can't be detected by visible signs."

Luke 17:20-21 NLT

Q: "Are You the King of the Jews?"
A: "You have said so."

Luke 23:3 ESV

Q: "How is it that this man has learning, when He has never studied?"
A: "My teaching is not Mine, but His who sent Me."

John 7:15-16 ESV

Q: "Where is Your Father?"
A: "You know neither Me nor My Father. If you had known Me, you would have known My Father also."

John 8:19 NKJV

Q: "Who are You?"
A: "Just what I have been saying to you from the beginning."

John 8:25 NKJV

Q: "How long will You keep us in suspense? If You are the Christ, tell us plainly."

A: "I told you, and you do not believe. The works that I do in My Father's name bear witness about Me, but you do not believe because you are not part of My flock."

John 10:24-26 ESV

Q: "Are You the King of the Jews?"

A: "My kingdom is not of this world. If My kingdom were of this world, My servants would fight, so that I should not be delivered to the Jews; but now My kingdom is not from here."

John 18:33, 36 NKJV

Questions from the Leaders

Q: "So You are a king?"

A: "You say that I am a king. For this purpose I was born and for this purpose I have come into the world."

John 18:37 ESV

Q: "Do You not know that I have power to crucify You, and power to release You?"

A: "You could have no power at all against Me unless it had been given you from above."

John 19:10-11 NKJV

Q: "Where did this man get this wisdom and these mighty works?"

A: "A prophet is not without honor except in his hometown and in his own household."

Matt. 13:54, 57 ESV

Q: "Teacher, what good deed must I do to have eternal life?"

A: "Why do you ask Me about what is good? There is only One who is good. If you would enter life, keep the commandments."

Matt. 19:16-17 ESV

Questions from People to Jesus

Q: "What else must I do?"

A: "If you want to be perfect, go and sell all your possessions and give the money to the poor, and you will have treasure in heaven. Then come, follow Me."

Matt. 19:20-21 NLT

Q: "Lord, are only a few people going to be saved?"

A: "Make every effort to enter through the narrow door, because many, I tell you, will try to enter and will not be able to."

Luke 13:23-24 NIV

Q: "Do we not say rightly that You are a Samaritan and have a demon?"

A: "I do not have a demon; but I honor My Father, and you dishonor Me."

John 8:48-49 NKJV

Q: "Who do You make Yourself out to be?"

A: "If I honor Myself, My honor is nothing. It is My Father who honors Me, of whom you say that He is your God. Yet you have not known Him, but I know Him. And if I say, 'I do not know Him,' I shall be a liar like you; but I do know Him and keep His word."

John 8:53-55 NKJV

Questions from People to Jesus

Q: "You are not yet fifty years old, and have You seen Abraham?"

A: "Before Abraham was, I am."

John 8:57-58 ESV

Q: "We understood from Scripture that the Messiah would live forever. How can You say the Son of Man will die? Just who is this Son of Man, anyway?"

A: "My light will shine for you just a little longer. Walk in the light while you can, so the darkness will not overtake you. Those who walk in the darkness cannot see where they are going. Put your trust in the light while there is still time; then you will become children of the light."

John 12:34-36 NLT

Q: "Who do people say that the Son of Man is?"
A: "Some say John the Baptist, others say Elijah, and others Jeremiah or one of the prophets."

Matt. 16:13-14 ESV

Q: "Who do you say that I am?"
A: "You are the Christ, the Son of the living God."

Matt. 16:15-16 ESV

Questions from Jesus to People

Q: "Many good works I have shown you from My Father. For which of those works do you stone Me?"

A: "For a good work we do not stone You, but for blasphemy, and because You, being a Man, make Yourself God."

John 10:32-33 NKJV

Q: "Who is My mother and who are My brothers?"

A: Here are My mother and My brothers! For whoever does the will of My Father in heaven is My brother and sister and mother."

Matt. 12:48-50 NKJV

JESUS' WORDS FOR DAILY LIVING

Acceptance

....

"Don't hesitate to accept hospitality, because those who work deserve to be fed."

Matt. 10:10 NLT

"No prophet is accepted in his own country."

Luke 4:24 NKJV

"Anyone who accepts your message is also accepting Me. And anyone who rejects you is rejecting Me. And anyone who rejects Me is rejecting God, who sent Me."

Luke 10:16 NLT

"I do not accept glory from human beings."

John 5:41 NIV

"I have come in My Father's name, and you do not accept Me; but if someone else comes in his own name, you will accept him."

John 5:43 NIV

"However, those the Father has given Me will come to Me, and I will never reject them."

John 6:37 NLT

"Receive the Holy Spirit."

John 20:22 ESV

Adultery

"Everyone who looks at a woman with lustful intent has already committed adultery with her in his heart."

Matt. 5:28 ESV

"A man who divorces his wife, unless she has been unfaithful, causes her to commit adultery. And anyone who marries a divorced woman also commits adultery."

Matt. 5:32 NLT

"Whoever divorces his wife and marries another commits adultery against her. And if a woman divorces her husband and marries another, she commits adultery."

Mark 10:11-12 NKJV

"Blessed are you when people insult you, persecute you and falsely say all kinds of evil against you because of Me."

Matt. 5:11 NIV

"Don't do your good deeds publicly, to be admired by others."

Matt. 6:1 NLT

"Only those who actually do the will of My Father in heaven will enter."

Matt. 7:21 NLT

"Why do you entertain evil thoughts in your hearts?"

Matt. 9:4 NIV

Character

"He who endures to the end will be saved."
Matt. 10:22 NKJV

"On the day of judgment people will give account for every careless word they speak."
Matt. 12:36 ESV

"By your words you will be justified, and by your words you will be condemned."
Matt. 12:37 NKJV

"It is from within, out of a person's heart, that evil thoughts come."

Mark 7:21 NIV

"The good person out of the good treasure of his heart produces good, and the evil person out of his evil treasure produces evil, for out of the abundance of the heart his mouth speaks."

Luke 6:45 ESV

"Let him who is without sin among you be the first to throw a stone."

John 8:7 ESV

Comfort

"Come to Me, all you who are weary and burdened, and I will give you rest. Take My yoke upon you and learn from Me, for I am gentle and humble in heart, and you will find rest for your souls. For My yoke is easy and My burden is light."

Matt. 11:28-30 NIV

"Where two or three are gathered in My name, there am I among them."

Matt. 18:20 ESV

"Everyone who acknowledges Me before men, the Son of Man also will acknowledge before the angels of God."

Luke 12:8 ESV

"Consider how the wild flowers grow. They do not labor or spin. Yet I tell you, not even Solomon in all his splendor was dressed like one of these. If that is how God clothes the grass of the field, which is here today, and tomorrow is thrown into the fire, how much more will He clothe you."

Luke 12:27-28 NIV

"I am leaving you with a gift – peace of mind and heart. And the peace I give is a gift the world cannot give. So don't be troubled or afraid."

John 14:27 NLT

"He who believes and is baptized will be saved; but he who does not believe will be condemned."

Mark 16:16 NKJV

"How can you escape the condemnation of hell?"

Matt. 23:33 NKJV

"Every tree that does not bear good fruit is cut down and thrown into the fire."

Matt. 7:19 NKJV

"Whoever believes in Him is not condemned, but whoever does not believe is condemned already, because He has not believed in the name of the only Son of God."

John 3:18 ESV

"And this is the condemnation, that the light has come into the world, and men loved darkness rather than light, because their deeds were evil."

John 3:19 NKJV

Courage

"In this world you will have trouble. But take heart! I have overcome the world."

John 16:33 NIV

"The spirit indeed is willing, but the flesh is weak."

Matt. 26:41 ESV

"Take courage! I am here!"

Mark 6:50 NLT

"If you have faith and don't doubt, you can do things like this and much more."

Matt. 21:21 NLT

"Why are you so afraid? Have you still no faith?"

Mark 4:40 ESV

"Do not fear, only believe."

Mark 5:36 ESV

Doubt

"If anyone says to this mountain, 'Go, throw yourself into the sea,' and does not doubt in their heart but believes that what they say will happen, it will be done for them."

Mark 11:23 NIV

"Whatever you ask in prayer, believe that you have received it, and it will be yours."

Mark 11:24 ESV

"Don't let your hearts be troubled. Trust in God, and trust also in Me."

John 14:1 NLT

"Because you believed, it has happened."

Matt. 8:13 NLT

"Because of your faith, it will happen."

Matt. 9:29 NLT

"Great is your faith! Be it done for you as you desire."

Matt. 15:28 ESV

"If you had faith even as small as a mustard seed, you could say to this mountain, 'Move from here to there,' and it would move. Nothing would be impossible."

Matt. 17:20 NLT

Faith

"If you have faith and don't doubt, you can do things like this and much more."

Matt. 21:21 NLT

"If you believe, you will receive whatever you ask for in prayer."

Matt. 21:22 NIV

"Why are you so afraid? Have you still no faith?"

Mark 4:40 ESV

"Don't be afraid. Just have faith."

Mark 5:36 NLT

"Anything is possible if a person believes."

Mark 9:23 NLT

"All things are possible with God."

Mark 10:27 ESV

"Have faith in God."

Mark 11:22 NKJV

"If anyone says to this mountain, 'Go, throw yourself into the sea,' and does not doubt in their heart but believes that what they say will happen, it will be done for them."

Mark 11:23 NIV

"You can pray for anything, and if you believe that you've received it, it will be yours."

Mark 11:24 NLT

"I have not found such great faith even in Israel."

Luke 7:9 NIV

"Your faith has saved you. Go in peace."

Luke 7:50 NKJV

"If I have told you earthly things and you do not believe, how can you believe if I tell you heavenly things?"

John 3:12 ESV

"Will you never believe in Me unless you see miraculous signs and wonders?"

John 4:48 NLT

"Believe in the one He has sent."

John 6:29 NIV

"He who believes in Me has everlasting life."

John 6:47 NKJV

Faith

"Whoever believes in Me, as Scripture has said, rivers of living water will flow from within them."

John 7:38 NIV

"Believe in God; believe also in Me."

John 14:1 ESV

"Believe because of the work you have seen Me do."

John 14:11 NLT

"Whoever believes in Me will do the works I have been doing, and they will do even greater things than these."

John 14:12 NIV

"Stop doubting and believe."

John 20:27 NIV

"Blessed are those who have not seen and yet have believed."

John 20:29 NIV

Fear

"Don't be afraid. Take courage! I am here!"

Mark 6:50 NLT

"Do not be afraid."

Matt 14:27 ESV

"Have no fear."

Matt 17:7 ESV

"Fear God, who has the power to kill you and then throw you into hell."

Luke 12:5 NLT

"Do not be afraid, but go on speaking and do not be silent, for I am with you, and no one will attack you to harm you."

Acts 18:9-10 ESV

"Do not be afraid; I am the First and the Last."

Rev. 1:17 NKJV

"Do not fear any of those things which you are about to suffer."

Rev. 2:10 NKJV

"Don't be afraid. From now on you'll be fishing for people!"

Luke 5:10 NLT

Forgiveness

"If you forgive those who sin against you, your heavenly Father will forgive you."

Matt. 6:14 NLT

"Be encouraged, My child! Your sins are forgiven."

Matt. 9:2 NLT

"If you do not forgive others their trespasses, neither will your Father forgive your trespasses."

Matt. 6:15 ESV

"This is My blood of the covenant, which is poured out for many for the forgiveness of sins."

Matt. 26:28 ESV

"All sins will be forgiven the children of man, and whatever blasphemies they utter."

Mark 3:28 ESV

"Forgive, and you will be forgiven."

Luke 6:37 NKJV

Forgiveness

"Father, forgive them, for they don't know what they are doing."

Luke 23:34 NLT

"If your brother or sister sins against you, rebuke them; and if they repent, forgive them. Even if they sin against you seven times in a day and seven times come back to you saying 'I repent,' you must forgive them."

Luke 17:3-4 NIV

"There is forgiveness of sins for all who repent."

Luke 24:47 NLT

"If you forgive anyone's sins, their sins are forgiven; if you do not forgive them, they are not forgiven."

John 20:23 NIV

"They will receive forgiveness for their sins and be given a place among God's people, who are set apart by faith in Me."

Acts 26:18 NLT

"Forgive us our sins, as we have forgiven those who sin against us."

Matt. 6:12 NLT

Fruitfulness

....

"Remain in Me, as I also remain in you. No branch can bear fruit by itself; it must remain in the vine. Neither can you bear fruit unless you remain in Me."

John 15:4 NIV

"By this My Father is glorified, that you bear much fruit."

John 15:8 NKJV

"You didn't choose Me. I chose you. I appointed you to go and produce lasting fruit."

John 15:16 NLT

"Every good tree bears good fruit, but a bad tree bears bad fruit. A good tree cannot bear bad fruit, and a bad tree cannot bear good fruit."

Matt. 7:17-18 NIV

"Every tree that does not bear good fruit is cut down and thrown into the fire. Thus, by their fruit you will recognize them."

Matt. 7:19-20 NIV

"A tree is identified by its fruit. If a tree is good, its fruit will be good. If a tree is bad, its fruit will be bad."

Matt. 12:33 NLT

Generosity

....

"Give to those who ask, and don't turn away from those who want to borrow."

Matt. 5:42 NLT

"When you do a charitable deed, do not let your left hand know what your right hand is doing, that your charitable deed may be in secret; and your Father who sees in secret will Himself reward you openly."

Matt. 6:3-4 NKJV

"Where your treasure is, there your heart will be also."

Matt. 6:21 NKJV

"Freely you have received, freely give."

Matt. 10:8 NKJV

"Be merciful, just as your Father is merciful."

Luke 6:36 NIV

"Give, and it will be given to you: good measure, pressed down, shaken together, and running over will be put into your bosom. For with the same measure that you use, it will be measured back to you."

Luke 6:38 NKJV

Generosity
....

"Be generous to the poor, and everything will be clean for you."

Luke 11:41 NIV

"Beware! Guard against every kind of greed. Life is not measured by how much you own."

Luke 12:15 NLT

"Use worldly wealth to gain friends for yourselves, so that when it is gone, you will be welcomed into eternal dwellings."

Luke 16:9 NIV

"If the world hates you, remember that it hated Me first."

John 15:18 NLT

"Whoever hates Me hates My Father also."

John 15:23 ESV

"The world cannot hate you, but it hates Me because I testify of it that its works are evil."

John 7:7 NKJV

"Be healed!"

Matt. 8:3 NLT

"I will come and heal him."

Matt. 8:7 NKJV

"Your faith has healed you."

Matt. 9:22 NIV

"Your faith has made you well; go in peace, and be healed of your disease."

Mark 5:34 ESV

"Healthy people don't need a doctor – sick people do."

Luke 5:31 NLT

"I will keep on driving out demons and healing people today and tomorrow."

Luke 13:32 NIV

"Sickness will not end in death. No, it is for God's glory so that God's Son may be glorified through it."

John 11:4 NIV

Heaven and Hell

"If you curse someone, you are in danger of the fires of hell."

Matt. 5:22 NLT

"You can enter God's Kingdom only through the narrow gate. The highway to hell is broad, and its gate is wide for the many who choose that way."

Matt. 7:13 NLT

"The Son of Man will send out His angels, and they will gather out of His Kingdom all things that offend, and those who practice lawlessness, and will cast them into the furnace of fire. There will be wailing and gnashing of teeth."

Matt. 13:41-42 NKJV

"Then the King will turn to those on the left and say, 'Away with you, you cursed ones, into the eternal fire prepared for the devil and his demons."

Matt. 25:41 NLT

"It's better to enter eternal life with only one hand than to go into the unquenchable fires of hell with two hands."

Mark 9:43 NLT

"If your eye causes you to sin, gouge it out. It's better to enter the Kingdom of God with only one eye than to have two eyes and be thrown into hell."

Mark 9:47 NLT

"It's better to enter eternal life with only one foot than to be thrown into hell with two feet."

Mark 9:45 NLT

"If you do not remain in Me, you are like a branch that is thrown away and withers; such branches are picked up, thrown into the fire and burned."

John 15:6 NIV

"Let what you say be simply 'Yes' or 'No'; anything more than this comes from evil."

Matt. 5:37 ESV

"One who is dishonest in a very little is also dishonest in much."

Luke 16:10 ESV

"When the Spirit of truth comes, He will guide you into all the truth."

John 16:13 ESV

"Give as freely as you have received."

Matt. 10:8 NLT

"Don't hesitate to accept hospitality, because those who work deserve to be fed."

Matt. 10:10 NLT

"Whatever you did for one of the least of these brothers and sisters of Mine, you did for Me."

Matt. 25:40 NIV

"Anyone who gives you a cup of water in My name because you belong to the Messiah will certainly not lose their reward."

Mark 9:41 NIV

"When you give a feast, invite the poor, the crippled, the lame, the blind, and you will be blessed, because they cannot repay you."

Luke 14:13-14 ESV

Humility

"God blesses those who are humble, for they will inherit the whole earth."
Matt. 5:5 NLT

"Anyone who becomes as humble as this little child is the greatest in the Kingdom of Heaven."
Matt. 18:4 NLT

"Whoever wants to be a leader among you must be your servant."
Matt. 20:26 NLT

"God blesses those who are humble."

Matt. 5:5 NLT

"The greatest among you shall be your servant."

Matt. 23:11 ESV

"Whoever exalts himself will be humbled, and whoever humbles himself will be exalted."

Matt. 23:12 ESV

"What is highly esteemed among men is an abomination in the sight of God."

Luke 16:15 NKJV

Humility

"When someone invites you to a wedding feast, do not take the place of honor, for a person more distinguished than you may have been invited. If so, the host who invited both of you will come and say to you, 'Give this person your seat.' Then, humiliated, you will have to take the least important place. But when you are invited, take the lowest place, so that when your host comes, he will say to you, 'Friend, move up to a better place.' Then you will be honored in the presence of all the other guests."

Luke 14:8-10 NIV

"When you fast, do not be like the hypocrites, with a sad countenance. For they disfigure their faces that they may appear to men to be fasting. Assuredly, I say to you, they have their reward. But you, when you fast, anoint your head and wash your face, so that you do not appear to men to be fasting."

Matt. 6:16-18 NKJV

Hypocrisy

"The teachers of the law and the Pharisees sit in Moses' seat. So you must be careful to do everything they tell you. But do not do what they do, for they do not practice what they preach. They tie up heavy, cumbersome loads and put them on other people's shoulders, but they themselves are not willing to lift a finger to move them."

Matt. 23:2-4 NIV

"Woe to you, teachers of the law and Pharisees, you hypocrites! You shut the door of the kingdom of heaven in people's faces. You yourselves do not enter, nor will you let those enter who are trying to."

Matt. 23:13 NIV

"What sorrow awaits you teachers of religious law and you Pharisees. Hypocrites! For you are careful to tithe even the tiniest income from your herb gardens, but you ignore the more important aspects of the law – justice, mercy, and faith. You should tithe, yes, but do not neglect the more important things. Blind guides!"

Matt. 23:23-24 NLT

Hypocrisy

"Woe to you, teachers of the law and Pharisees, you hypocrites! You are like whitewashed tombs, which look beautiful on the outside but on the inside are full of the bones of the dead and everything unclean. In the same way, on the outside you appear to people as righteous but on the inside you are full of hypocrisy and wickedness."

Matt. 23:27-28 NIV

"Rejoice and be glad, for your reward is great in heaven."

Matt. 5:12 ESV

"Blessed are you who weep now, for you will laugh."

Luke 6:21 NIV

"Be happy! Yes, leap for joy! For a great reward awaits you in heaven."

Luke 6:23 NLT

"What sorrow awaits you who are rich, for you have your only happiness now."

Luke 6:24 NLT

"Rejoice because your names are written in heaven."

Luke 10:20 NKJV

"I have told you these things so that you will be filled with My joy. Yes, your joy will overflow!"

John 15:11 NIV

"I say to you that you will weep and lament, but the world will rejoice; and you will be sorrowful, but your sorrow will be turned into joy."

John 16:20 NKJV

"Anyone who is angry with a brother or sister will be subject to judgment."

Matt. 5:22 NIV

"If you had known what this means, 'I desire mercy, and not sacrifice,' you would not have condemned the guiltless."

Matt. 12:7 ESV

"By your words you will be acquitted, and by your words you will be condemned."

Matt. 12:37 NIV

"With the measure you use, it will be measured to you – and even more."

Mark 4:24 NIV

"Do not judge others, and you will not be judged."

Luke 6:37 NLT

"Do not judge by appearances, but judge with right judgment."

John 7:24 ESV

"Let the one who has never sinned throw the first stone!"

John 8:7 NLT

"Will not God bring about justice for His chosen ones, who cry out to Him day and night? Will He keep putting them off? I tell you, He will see that they get justice, and quickly."

Luke 18:7-8 NIV

"Come to terms quickly with your accuser while you are going with him to court."

Matt. 5:25 ESV

"You will be acting as true children of your Father in heaven. For He gives His sunlight to both the evil and the good, and He sends rain on the just and the unjust alike."

Matt. 5:45 NLT

"By your words you will be justified, and by your words you will be condemned."

Matt. 12:37 ESV

"You neglect justice and the love of God."

Luke 11:42 NIV

"Let the one who has never sinned throw the first stone!"

John 8:7 NLT

"Put your sword in its place, for all who take the sword will perish by the sword."

Matt. 26:52 NKJV

"Whoever loses their life for Me and for the gospel will save it."

Mark 8:35 NIV

"Whoever wants to save their life will lose it, but whoever loses their life for Me will save it."

Luke 9:24 NIV

Life and Death

"I have come that they may have life, and have it to the full."

John 10:10 NIV

"God so loved the world that He gave His only begotten Son, that whoever believes in Him should not perish but have everlasting life."

John 3:16 NKJV

"Whoever hears My word and believes Him who sent Me has eternal life and will not be judged."

John 5:24 NIV

"It is the Spirit who gives life."

John 6:63 NKJV

"Unless you believe that I am He you will die in your sins."

John 8:24 ESV

"Whoever obeys My word will never see death."

John 8:51 NIV

Light and Darkness

"I am the light of the world. Whoever follows Me will not walk in darkness, but will have the light of life."

John 8:12 ESV

"As long as I am in the world, I am the light of the world."

John 9:5 NKJV

"I have come into the world as light, so that whoever believes in Me may not remain in darkness."

John 12:46 ESV

"The lamp of the body is the eye. If therefore your eye is good, your whole body will be full of light. But if your eye is bad, your whole body will be full of darkness. If therefore the light that is in you is darkness, how great is that darkness!"

Matt. 6:22-23 NKJV

"Whatever I tell you in the dark, speak in the light; and what you hear in the ear, preach on the housetops."

Matt. 10:27 NKJV

"Make sure that the light you think you have is not actually darkness."

Luke 11:35 NLT

Light and Darkness

"Would anyone light a lamp and the put it under a basket or under a bed? Of course not! A lamp is placed on a stand, where its light will shine."

Mark 4:21 NLT

"If your whole body is full of light, and no part of it dark, it will be just as full of light as when a lamp shines its light on you."

Luke 11:36 NIV

"Light has come into the world, but people loved darkness instead of light because their deeds were evil."

John 3:19 NIV

"Love your enemies and pray for those who persecute you."

Matt. 5:44 ESV

"Love your neighbor as yourself."

Matt. 22:39 NKJV

"Bless those who curse you, and pray for those who spitefully use you."

Luke 6:28 NKJV

"Do to others as you would have them do to you."

Luke 6:31 NIV

Love

_____

"Love your enemies! Do good to them."

Luke 6:35 NLT

"Your love for one another will prove to the world that you are My disciples."

John 13:35 NLT

"Love one another as I have loved you."

John 15:12 NKJV

"Everyone who looks at a woman with lustful intent has already committed adultery with her in his heart."

Matt. 5:28 ESV

"A man who divorces his wife, unless she has been unfaithful, causes her to commit adultery. And anyone who marries a divorced woman also commits adultery."

Matt. 5:32 NLT

Marriage and Divorce

"A man will leave his father and mother and be united to his wife, and the two will become one flesh. So they are no longer two, but one flesh. Therefore what God has joined together, let no one separate."

Mark 10:7-9 NIV

"Whoever divorces his wife and marries another commits adultery against her. And if a woman divorces her husband and marries another, she commits adultery."

Mark 10:11-12 NKJV

"Marriage is for people here on earth."

Luke 20:34 NLT

"Blessed are the merciful, for they shall receive mercy."

Matt. 5:7 ESV

"I desire mercy, and not sacrifice."

Matt. 12:7 ESV

"Be merciful, just as your Father is merciful."

Luke 6:36 NIV

Money and Possessions

"Don't store up treasures here on earth, where moths eat them and rust destroys them, and where thieves break in and steal. Store your treasures in heaven, where moths and rust cannot destroy, and thieves do not break in and steal."

Matt. 6:19-20 NLT

"You cannot serve God and money."

Matt. 6:24 ESV

"I will give you the keys of the kingdom of heaven, and whatever you bind on earth will be bound in heaven, and whatever you loose on earth will be loosed in heaven."

Matt. 16:19 NKJV

"What will it profit a man if he gains the whole world and forfeits his soul?

Matt. 16:26 ESV

"Whatever you bind on earth shall be bound in heaven, and whatever you loose on earth shall be loosed in heaven."

Matt. 18:18 ESV

"It is hard for someone who is rich to enter the kingdom of heaven."

Matt. 19:23 NIV

"It is easier for a camel to go through the eye of a needle than for a rich man to enter the kingdom of God."

Matt. 19:24 NKJV

"Everyone who has given up houses or brothers or sisters or father or mother or children or property, for My sake, will receive a hundred times as much in return and will inherit eternal life."

Matt. 19:29 NLT

"Go and sell all your possessions and give the money to the poor, and you will have treasure in heaven."

Mark 10:21 NLT

"What sorrow awaits you who are rich, for you have your only happiness now."

Luke 6:24 NLT

"To the one who has, more will be given, and from the one who has not, even what he thinks that he has will be taken away."

Luke 8:18 ESV

"Beware! Guard against every kind of greed. Life is not measured by how much you own."

Luke 12:15 NLT

"Sell your possessions, and give to the needy."

Luke 12:33 ESV

"Where your treasure is, there your heart will be also."

Luke 12:34 NKJV

"You cannot become My disciple without giving up everything you own."

Luke 14:33 NLT

"You will always have the poor among you, but you will not always have Me."

John 12:8 NLT

"If anyone forces you to go one mile, go with them two miles."

Matt. 5:41 NIV

"Not everyone who says to Me, 'Lord, Lord,' will enter the kingdom of heaven, but the one who does the will of My Father who is in heaven."

Matt. 7:21 ESV

"Whoever has ears, let them hear."

Matt. 13:9 NIV

"If you abide in My word, you are My disciples indeed."

John 8:31 NKJV

"Whoever obeys My word will never see death."

John 8:51 NIV

"If you love Me, obey My commandments."

John 14:15 NLT

"Peace be with you. As the Father has sent Me, so I am sending you."

John 20:21 NLT

"Blessed are the peacemakers, for they will be called children of God."

Matt. 5:9 NIV

"Peace I leave with you, My peace I give to you."

John 14:27 NKJV

"I am leaving you with a gift – peace of mind and heart."

John 14:27 NLT

"Let your good deeds shine out for all to see, so that everyone will praise your heavenly Father."

Matt. 5:16 NLT

"Sickness will not end in death. No, it is for God's glory so that God's Son may be glorified through it."

John 11:4 NIV

"Father, glorify Your name."

John 12:28 NKJV

"The Son of Man is glorified, and God is glorified in Him. If God is glorified in Him, God will also glorify Him in Himself, and glorify Him immediately."

John 13:31-32 NKJV

"I will do whatever you ask in My name, so that the Father may be glorified in the Son."

John 14:13 NIV

"This is to My Father's glory, that you bear much fruit, showing yourselves to be My disciples."

John 15:8 NIV

......

"Judgment will fall on this very generation."

Matt. 23:36 NLT

"Someone who does not know, and then does something wrong, will be punished only lightly."

Luke 12:48 NLT

"I correct and discipline everyone I love."

Rev. 3:19 NLT

"Blessed are the pure in heart, for they shall see God."

Matt. 5:8 ESV

"Whoever does what is true comes to the light, so that it may be clearly seen that his works have been carried out in God."

John 3:21 ESV

"I know all the things you do. I have seen your love, your faith, your service, and your patient endurance."

Rev. 2:19 NLT

Renewal

"No one tears a piece out of a new garment to patch an old one. Otherwise, they will have torn the new garment, and the patch from the new will not match the old."

Luke 5:36 NIV

"No one pours new wine into old wineskins. Otherwise, the new wine will burst the skins; the wine will run out and the wineskins will be ruined. No, new wine must be poured into new wineskins."

Luke 5:37-38 NIV

"It is fitting for us to fulfill all righteousness."

Matt. 3:15 ESV

"Blessed are those who hunger and thirst for righteousness, for they shall be satisfied."

Matt. 5:6 ESV

"Blessed are those who are persecuted for righteousness' sake"

Matt. 5:10 ESV

Righteousness

"Unless your righteousness is better than the righteousness of the teachers of religious law and the Pharisees, you will never enter the Kingdom of Heaven!"

Matt. 5:20 NLT

"Beware of practicing your righteousness before other people in order to be seen by them, for then you will have no reward from your Father who is in heaven."

Matt. 6:1 ESV

"The righteous will shine like the sun in the kingdom of their Father."

Matt. 13:43 ESV

Your eye is the lamp of your body. When your eye is healthy, your whole body is full of light, but when it is bad, your body is full of darkness. Therefore be careful lest the light in you be darkness. If then your whole body is full of light, having no part dark, it will be wholly bright."

Luke 11:34-36 ESV

Servanthood

....

"The greatest among you must be a servant."

Matt. 23:11 NLT

"Anyone who wants to be the first must be the very last, and the servant of all."

Mark 9:35 NIV

"Be dressed for service and keep your lamps burning."

Luke 12:35 NLT

"Whoever serves Me must follow Me; and where I am, My servant also will be. My Father will honor the one who serves Me."

John 12:26 NIV

"A servant is not greater than his master."

John 15:20 NKJV

Sin

"If any one of you wants to be My follower, you must turn from your selfish ways, take up your cross, and follow Me."

Mark 8:34 NLT

"Out of the heart come evil thoughts – murder, adultery, sexual immorality, theft, false testimony, slander."

Matt. 15:19 NIV

"If your hand or foot causes you to sin, cut it off."

Matt. 18:8 NKJV

"If your eye causes you to sin, tear it out and throw it away."

Matt. 18:9 NKJV

"If you hold anything against anyone, forgive them, so that your Father in heaven may forgive you your sins."

Mark 11:25 NKJV

"Your sins are forgiven."

Luke 7:48 NKJV

"Whoever commits sin is a slave of sin."

John 8:34 NKJV

"The world's sin is that it refuses to believe in Me."

John 16:9 ESV

"Get up and pray, so that you will not give in to temptation."

Luke 22:46 NLT

"Temptations are inevitable, but what sorrow awaits the person who does the tempting."

Matt. 18:7 NLT

"Pray that you may not enter into temptation."

Luke 22:46 ESV

"Whoever gives one of these little ones only a cup of cold water in the name of a disciple, assuredly, I say to you, he shall by no means lose his reward."

Matt. 10:42 NKJV

"If you want to be perfect, go, sell what you have and give to the poor, and you will have treasure in heaven."

Matt. 19:21 NKJV

"Sell what you have and give alms; provide yourselves money bags which do not grow old, a treasure in the heavens that does not fail, where no thief approaches nor moth destroys. For where your treasure is, there your heart will be also."

Luke 12:33-34 NKJV

Trustworthiness

"You shall not swear falsely, but shall perform your oaths to the Lord."

Matt. 5:33 NKJV

"Let your 'Yes' be 'Yes,' and your 'No,' 'No.' "

Matt. 5:37 NKJV

"You shall not give false testimony."

Mark 10:19 NIV

"The people of this world are more shrewd in dealing with their own kind than are the people of the light."

Luke 16:8 NIV

"Whoever can be trusted with very little can also be trusted with much, and whoever is dishonest with very little will also be dishonest with much."

Luke 16:10 NIV

"But whoever does what is true comes to the light, so that it may be clearly seen that his works have been carried out in God."

John 3:21 ESV

"Moses did not give you the bread from heaven, but My Father gives you the true bread from heaven."

John 6:32 NKJV

"A person who seeks to honor the One who sent him speaks truth, not lies."

John 7:18 NLT

"You shall know the truth, and the truth shall make you free."

John 8:32 NKJV

"If I tell the truth, why do you not believe Me?"

John 8:46 NKJV

"When the Spirit of truth comes, He will guide you into all the truth."

John 16:13 ESV

"God is spirit, and those who worship Him must worship in spirit and truth."

John 4:24 ESV

"Everyone on the side of truth listens to Me."

John 18:37 NIV

"You shall know the truth, and the truth shall make you free."

John 8:32 NKJV

Understanding

"The closer you listen, the more understanding you will be given – and you will receive even more."

Mark 4:24 NLT

"To those who listen to My teaching, more understanding will be given. But for those who are not listening, even what little understanding they have will be taken away from them."

Mark 4:25 NLT

"Anyone who listens to My teaching and follows it is wise."

Matt. 7:24 NLT

"Anyone who hears My teaching and doesn't obey it is foolish."

Matt. 7:26 NLT

"I will give you a mouth and wisdom which all your adversaries will not be able to contradict or resist."

Luke 21:15 NKJV

Worry

"Do not worry about your life, what you will eat or drink; or about your body, what you will wear."

Matt. 6:25 NIV

"Don't worry about tomorrow, for tomorrow will bring its own worries."

Matt. 6:34 NLT

"Come to Me, all you who are weary and burdened, and I will give you rest."

Matt. 11:28 NIV

"Take My yoke upon you and learn from Me, for I am gentle and lowly in heart, and you will find rest for your souls."

Matt. 11:29 NKJV

"You are worried and upset about many things, but few things are needed – or indeed only one."

Luke 10:41-42 NIV

"Can all your worries add a single moment to your life?"

Luke 12:25 NLT

"Don't let your hearts be troubled. Trust in God, and trust also in Me."

John 14:1 NLT

Worship

....

"Worship the Lord your God, and serve Him only."

Matt. 4:10 NIV

"If they keep quiet, the stones will cry out."

Luke 19:40 NIV

"The hour is coming when you will neither on this mountain,
nor in Jerusalem, worship the Father."

John 4:21 NKJV

"You worship what you do not know; we know what we worship, for salvation is of the Jews."

John 4:22 NKJV

"True worshipers will worship the Father in spirit and truth; for the Father is seeking such to worship Him."

John 4:23 NKJV

"God is spirit, and those who worship Him must worship in spirit and truth."

John 4:24 ESV

Index